The Midlife Money Playbook:

Get Ahead Financially and Stop Living Paycheck to Paycheck

The Midlife Career Change Playbook

A 12-Month Strategy to Replace Your Income and Live the Life of Your Dreams Without Risking Everything You Worked For

Table of Contents

Passive Income

7 Predictable Ways to Generate a Passive Income Stream when you are over 40 and While Working a Full Time Job

Table of Contents

High Income Producing Skills

7 Skills And Habits That Will Generate A 6 Figure Income

Table of Contents

The Midlife Career Change Playbook

A 12-Month Strategy to Replace Your Income and Live the Life of Your Dreams Without Risking Everything You Worked For

Table of Contents

inconvenience caused as a result of reliance on information as published on, or linked to, this book.

The author of this book has taken careful measures to share vital information about the subject. May its readers acquire the right knowledge, wisdom, **inspiration, and succeed.**

Introduction

Congratulations on downloading this book and thank you for doing so. If you are sick of your 9-5 office job and the daily grind, or if you are simply feeling unfulfilled and trapped in your current situation, then this book is for you. One thing that you should know is that you are not alone. The world is full of people who are unhappy and unsatisfied with their jobs. Needless to say, this has a bad impact on the quality of life. The good news is that there is a way out of this. You can make a difference as long as you put your heart into it. You have the power to make positive changes in your life.

Of course, this does not come without challenges. Although this may not be a problem if you are single, things are much different when you have certain responsibilities. For example, you may have a family to support and/or a mortgage to cover. Many things can happen in life. Now, some people shy away from doing what they want because of their responsibilities. They simply want to take the safest way, and that is to leave things as they are and stay unhappy every day. If you come to think about it, this does not solve anything. This book is not about taking the safest route in life. Rather, it encourages and teaches you to live the life that you want without being irresponsible. If you want to create positive and meaningful changes in your life, then you should work hard for it. If you want to have a career change without losing everything that you have already built so far, then this book will be your number one guide.

There are plenty of books about this subject in the market, thanks again for choosing this one! Every effort was made to ensure it is full of useful information. Please enjoy!

Step 1 — Build up 6 Months of Savings

What you intend to do demands more than careful planning. More importantly, it requires that you take actual steps and positive actions to achieve your goal. The first step is for you to start to build up 6 months' worth of savings. Actually, this is the first step towards a bigger goal. As the saying goes, "A journey of a thousand miles starts with a single step." This is that single step. Your objective is to be able to earn 6 months of savings. This is to ensure that you have enough money to support your family, as well as to cover for all your other expenses and obligations. Do not worry; you will most likely not spend all those savings. After all, you will also be making money along the way. However, this is important just to give you a good margin just in case the worst case happens where you fail and not earn any money. The amount of money that you need will depend on your needs. If you have a family to support, you will need more money, especially if you have several kids. You should always consider your situation. Be honest with your current financial standing. If you have debts and other obligations, then you should think of those things as well. This is an important part as it will give you a sense of direction, as well as the right action plan that you'll be taking. After all, the things that you have to do will also be influenced by your current financial situation.

There is no easier and quicker way to "earn" money than by saving money. By cutting down on your expenses, you can significantly increase the money that you have. Not knowing how to control your expenses, regardless if you're a high-income earner, you'll most likely end up in financial difficulty. Let us now look at some money-saving techniques and tips that you can do

The importance of living below your means

Whether you intend to quit your job or not, it is always important to learn to live below your means. Unfortunately, many people live above or beyond what they are capable of, and so they end up with lots of debts and all other bills and obligations that they could not resolve. Needless to say, you should never let this happen to you. If you want to have a successful, fulfilling, and happy life, then you should learn to live below your means. Now, do not think of this as something negative or that you would have to live poorly. This simply means that you need to ensure that your expenses are proportionate to your earnings. Anything that exceeds your income would mean that you will have some form of liability one way or another. Being able to live below your means is one of the best ways to save money.

It is also worth noting that you should strive to live *below* your means. This means that you need to have some excess after you have deducted your expenses. You have to be able to save money at least every month after paying for all your financial obligations. If you do not have savings, then that is something that has to be addressed quickly. It is advised that you get a pen and paper and list down your sources of income and expenses. Be specific as possible, especially when it comes to noting down your expenses. Once you have everything written down on paper, you should examine your list of expenses and think of ways on how you can minimize them. Is there something that you could drop from the list? Also, try to find out if there are more affordable alternatives for some of the items on your list. The key is to try to lower your expenses as much as possible. Take note that this does not mean that you have to live a poor and sad life. You can still buy whatever you want and enjoy life. But, you need to make it a priority to have some savings. Do not forget that this is your objective to earn enough savings that will support you for 6 months. This is not a simple task to accomplish especially if you have not yet saved any money or if your current earning is just exactly enough to pay for all of your needs.

The next step is to focus on your sources of income. Can you think of a way to increase your monthly income? With more income, you can also enjoy more savings. Do not worry; we will discuss notable ways to increase your income later in the book. Indeed, it is not unusual to find people who need to supplement their income just to earn enough money.

A common mistake is to increase one's expenses as the income increases. This is wrong. In fact, you should always try to cut down your expenses all the time. Focus on increasing your income and your savings. Once you are able to do this and you are able to generate enough money that can cover you for 6 months, then you can easily make decisions and take risks.

Next, you should compare your earnings versus your expenses. This involves just a bit of math. Simply subtract your total monthly expenses from your total monthly income. You should end up with a positive profit. If you get a negative number, then it means that your expenses are higher than your earnings – an easy and sure way to be in debt and financial distress. Hence, if you ever encountered this situation, you should do everything that you can to lower your expenses. Of course, you should also try to increase your income if you can. Still, the easiest and quickest way would simply be too cut down your expenses. If you really think about it, a person does not really need much to live a decent life. But, of course, things can be challenging when you have a family to support and a house to maintain, among others. If you know that your income is not enough, then talk to your family and decide on ways to lower the expenses. Do not be stressed out. I assure you, there are many people out there who are in far worse financial situation than you are, and yet they are able to survive and face life's challenges. It is all a matter of how well you handle these problems.

Again, if you want to save more money, then the best and easiest way to deal with it is by lowering your expenses. If you check your grocery list, you will definitely find some things that you have been buying but do not really need. There are also things that you do and spend money on that are not really essential. It is recommended that you write everything down on paper so that you could examine the situation from a clearer perspective. Again, the key is to lower your expenses to save more money. No matter what you do, you will not be able to give yourself a chance to live the life that you have always wanted unless you get to live lower than your means. Hence, this first step is a very important one that you should not take it for granted.

Money saving tips and techniques

Saving money is not hard or complicated at all. However, take note that you do need to make some sacrifices. The truth is that you do not need a lot just to survive. There are some people out there who have proven this by living off of a mere backpack. Of course, you do not need to take extreme measures just to save money, but the point here is that you do not have to spend so much unless you can really afford it.

Saving money only requires some adjustments. For example, instead of driving to and from work that is only a few kilometers away from your house all the time, you can just ride a bike and save the money that you normally use for your gas expense. If you think about it, this is not really a bad thing but a mere change in lifestyle. In fact, this can even be seen as a healthier lifestyle. Not only can you save more money, but it can also make you much healthier. Not to mention, it can be a very fun experience. Another example is instead of hiring a helper, you might want to be more responsible and clean the house yourself. This will also give you more privacy. As you can see, every change also has its positive side. At the same time, it allows you to earn money. Another example: Instead of using air conditioning, you might just use an electric fan from time to time. After all, a fan is more natural and can significantly lower your expenses. If you are fond of eating several big meals a day, maybe it is time for you to be healthy and go on a diet. Instead of eating and paying for several heavy meals, you might want to order smaller meals. Of course, this is not limited to just yourself, you can include the whole family. You do not just enjoy a healthier life, but you can also save more money. By making simple adjustments, you can effectively lower your costs and save more money. This is important for you to reach your objective of earning at least 6 months of money on savings.

Saving money by lowering your expenses does not always have to give you some form of inconvenience. Many times, it is simply important for you to realize that there are things that you are spending money on that you do not even need. It might just take some time for you to adjust, but it is nonetheless doable. You should learn to prioritize and be responsible. This is also a good way for you to realize that life means so much more than material things and wealth. However, you should not lower your cost to the point that it will give you a hard time. If you cannot make adjustments and lower your cost on one thing, you can just make adjustments on other things.

Saving money can even be fun. It sometimes depends on how you view certain changes. Some people find a better lifestyle when they try to save money. There are those who suddenly learn to appreciate the beauty of minimalism or even frugal living. After all, life itself is also an article, and you have the freedom on how you want to live your life. Just because you have money does not mean that you should live in a certain way. You always have a choice in how you live.

Saving on housing, transportation, and food expenses

Housing, transportation, and food – these three things normally constitute the biggest part of your expenses, since they are essential to living a good life. With the right attitude and approach, you can also cut down your costs on these things and save more money.

As for the housing, you do not need to live in a big and grand house right away. Such luxury can wait! As long as it has enough room to accommodate you and your family, then that would be fine. You should also be careful in choosing the location. Ideally, your house should be near your place of work. Time is an essential element. Not to mention, if you live far from your place of work, you will have to spend more money on gas. Indeed, time is money so you would not want to waste hours of time just commuting to work. You should train yourself to be productive at all times and increase efficiency.

Before you pay or enter into any contract, negotiate for the best deal. Have several good choices and compare them. When it comes to housing, you need to be very careful as it often involves a big expense.

Regarding transportation, you might want to look for an alternative such walking your way to work or riding a bike. Sometimes it is also better to commute than to bring your own car. This will depend on the circumstances of your situation.

Lowering your expenses is easy, yet it can significantly help you in raising money on savings. This is also something that you can start doing now. So, if you have not done it yet, it is time for you to grab a pen and paper and tally your income and expenses. To be deserving of success, you should make decisions and sacrifices. Do not worry; this is only temporary. When making adjustments, you might experience some inconvenience, especially if you are used to a life where you spend lots of things to bring you comfort. You do not really have to sacrifice your comfort, but you will definitely encounter some uneasiness, especially if you have not yet adjusted to the new routine or set up.

Even though you want to minimize your expenses, take note that this does not mean that you are not allowed to enjoy some luxuries and joys in life. After all, you are still working, and you deserve to have fun. Just be responsible enough, and do not overspend. Always keep your objectives in mind and do everything that you can to succeed.

During this stage, you may have some realizations. Most people learn just how dependent they have been on the comforts that money has to offer. At the same time, they also realize that there are many things that they pay for that they do not actually need. In fact, there are even those who may feel a certain sense of freedom for not being too dependent on money. Indeed, sometimes it is money that can make you feel less free. When a person becomes a slave to money, you end up chasing after it that you forget to notice and appreciate the beauty of life. As the saying goes, "Stop and smell the flowers." By lowering your expenses, you find ways not to depend on money and become free. This is the time when you can stop and finally appreciate life as it is instead of having your mind bombarded with things or services that you have to buy yet you do not actually need. This does not mean that money is bad. Rather, you also need to understand how to spend it wisely. By identifying the things that you actually need from those that you just thought you needed, you can significantly lower your monthly expenses.

It is important to learn to focus and cut down your expenses on these three (housing, transportation, and food) things as they constitute the bulk of your regular expenses. If you can manage these things, then you can have control over your money. Remember never to exceed your means to avoid complications. If necessary, live a simple life. You need to be ready to make some sacrifices to achieve your objective. Do not worry; this is only for a temporary period. Once you reach your objective of having enough savings for 6 months, you can give yourself more flexibility, and it is actually the fruit of your labor since, by then, you can finally live the life that you have always wanted.

Now that you know how to lower your expenses and enjoy more savings effectively, it is time to focus on increasing your income.

Step 2 — Earn More Money

It is time to talk about a very interesting topic, and that is how you can earn more money. The more that you earn, the easier life will be. Discussing how to earn more money is not a strange subject. Almost all people think about how they can earn more, even the rich wants to increase their income. Also, it will be easier for you to reach your 6-month savings that you need if you are able to increase your income. Just be careful not to commit the mistake of also increasing your expenses when your income goes up. Of course, you can treat yourself and increase your expenses a little bit, but be sure to have a good control over it. What you need to focus on is increasing the amount of money that you can save every month. Some people feel even more motivated at this point and further cut down their expenses. Although this is a good thing, remember not to overdo it to the point that your family no longer feels comfortable. Keep in mind that saving money should not make you suffer. Doing simple adjustments should be enough.

When people want to earn money, many of them simply think about money. This is wrong. Instead, you should think about positive actions that you should do that will generate money. Money will not be generated without actions. Rather, you should view money as a product or fruit of something that you did. Hence, the best way to earn money is to think of ways of how you can be of service to people.

If you do this either by selling a product or offering a service, or even both, then you will be paid in money. This is how you actually make money. As you can see, it is different from simply thinking about money. If you want to earn money, then you should take actions and work for it.

Earning more money is actually what so many people want. From time to time, people wonder: How can I earn more money? This is also the reason why there are people who want to escape from their 9-5 job. This is true especially when they realize that their 9-5 job, secured as it may be, also limits their earning potential. When you have the usual office job, generally, you already know just how much you will earn in a month, even in a year. There is a fixed amount that you will get for all of your efforts. But, when you freelance or put up your own business, even if it is just an online business, you create an opportunity to earn more income, and the good news here is that there is no limit to how much you can earn. Of course, there are different ways to earn more money. Some may involve a simple increase in your current income from your job, yet it could still be very helpful to your current situation, while others might be riskier but with a higher earning potential.

So, how can you effectively increase your income and earn more money? Let us discuss the different ways that you can do to make this happen:

Get a promotion or a raise (even if you do not want to leave your job)

To boost your income, the most natural way would be to focus on the work that you already have. Take note that this does not mean that you should stick to your job, but at least use it to reach your objective of getting enough savings for six months. Do your best and try to get promoted. As you may already know, promotions are associated with an increase in the salary. Another option that you have is to talk with your boss and politely ask for a raise, if your boss is understanding enough, you can even explain your situation to him, and he might help you out. However, keep in mind that your boss is not obliged to give you a raise unless there are compelling legal reasons to do so; therefore, you should also learn to manage your expectations.

Of course, before you can expect to be promoted or given a raise, you should first deserve it. This is why you need to do your best at work, even if it is the work that you want to abandon later on. Still, it does not change the fact that at the present time, it is your current work that allows you to pay for the bills.

Learn the skills that your career teaches you. They may be useful in other things other than your current work. The work experience itself is also a rich source of knowledge. When you are used to working hard, then other kinds of work can soon be easy for you to do.

You have to understand that just because you want to change your job does not mean that you can just abandon your present work immediately. In fact, it may mean doing more on your present job to allow you to shift to a new job. You first need to have a strong foundation before you can safely take on a new route. This is important especially when other people depend on you for support. The good news is that it is something that *you* can do. It may just take more time and effort, but it is nonetheless doable, and you are the right person to make it happen.

Freelance (after hours of using the skills from your career)

Your present career will arm you with certain skills. These days, freelancing is getting popular. No, you do not need to leave your job and be a full-time freelancer. Although this is possible and there are people out there who have reported success by going freelancer on a full-time basis, it is still quite a risky venture, so you need to be careful with your decisions and actions. What you can do is to be a part-time freelancer. If you work during the day, you might want to handle some freelancer projects in the evening or over the weekends. One of the best things about freelancing is that you get to be in control of your time. Take note that just because you have more control of your time when you are a freelancer does not mean that you can just be lazy. Rather, you have to spend your time effectively and efficiently.

Freelancing is a good way to get more work, which means more money. If you are serious about boosting your present income, then this is definitely something that you might want to try.

Freelancing is fun. In fact, it is not unusual to find someone who simply tried freelancing but ended up doing it as the full-time job. Working as a freelancer gives you the opportunity to be your own boss and to set your own hours. You can even choose the client or projects that you want to work on. However, the challenge here is that you will be living from paycheck to paycheck. This means that if you stop working or if you run out of projects to work on, then you will also not get any income.

Start an online business: Kindle Publishing, blogging, affiliate marketing, etc.

Another thing that you can do is to engage in an online business. There are many people these days who are able to leave their day job and work full time in the comfort of their homes because of their online business. This is a good way for you to earn extra and passive income. In addition, this can be a fun activity that you can do after your office work. Since it simply involves an online presence, you can engage in this kind of business even in the comfort of your home. Now, there are many kinds of online business. Let us look at notable ways to earn money online:

➢ Kindle Publishing

This is one of the best ways to earn passive income online. You can write ebooks and publish them on Kindle. The ebooks will be sold at Amazon and other key book retailers online. What is an ebook? It is an electronic or digital format of a book; hence, it is called an *e-book*. Record shows that ebook sales on Amazon have now become higher than sales from traditionally published paperback books. Today, more and more people are learning to appreciate the value and benefits of using an ebook over a paperback book, such as being able to bring and access your ebooks anywhere you go, to avoid wear and tear, easy search feature, and others.

Some people have earned a high amount of income just by publishing ebooks. For publishing on Amazon, you might want to use KDP or Kindle Direct Publishing. This is the publishing platform of Amazon. When you publish using KDP, you get to distribute your ebooks not only to Amazon but also to other ebook channels. Why Amazon? Well, different cases show that Amazon has the biggest share in terms of ebook sales. This is because Amazon has well established itself in the market with millions of loyal and active customers. If you write good ebooks, you will definitely have a market for your product.

You can also come up with a physical, paperback copy of your ebooks by going to *Createspace*. Createspace is also owned by Amazon. It is the publishing platform that will allow you to do publish your book in a paperback format. It is also worth noting that both KDP and Createspace are free to use.

So, just how much can you make? Well, there are no hard and fast rules on this matter. There are ebook sellers out there who barely earn anything, while there are also those who earn thousands of dollars, and even a fortune, from their ebooks. You should approach this as a business where your ebook is your product.

Now, a common problem that people face when they use this approach is that they are not confident of their writing. After all, before you can have an ebook that you can sell, you need to write a book. This is easy if you are fond of writing, but what if you are one of the many people out there who simply have no interest or time to write? Well, do not worry; this may surprise you, but the truth is that there are many ebook sellers out there who do not write. How is this possible? The way to do this is to hire a ghostwriter to write your book. A ghostwriter will do the work of writing your book for you. When you hire a ghostwriter, you remain as the sole author of the book. Your ghostwriter will not have any credit as long as you pay him to write your book. You can find affordable ghostwriting services from content mills like Upwork or Freelancer. However, just a word of caution: Stay away from ghostwriters that offer their services for a very low price as they tend to have low-quality work as well. Now, the ghostwriting rates vary greatly. You can find a ghostwriter to write your book for $200, but there are also those who would charge thousands of dollars for their service. If you want a highly professional quality of work, then you might want to pay for a more experienced ghostwriter. However, expect the fee to be higher than usual. To make money out of selling ebooks, you do not really need to hire a highly professional ghostwriter. You can stick to ghostwriters that will charge a few hundred dollars for a book. The important thing is to have a work that has a decent quality.

You may not be aware of this, but more than 60% of published books are written by ghostwriters. Some of the books in the bestsellers list were also made by professional ghostwriters. When it comes to the business of making money by selling ebooks, you will find that hiring several ghostwriters to write ebooks for you can be helpful. However, you should be careful with your budget. Be sure to manage your money properly. You can start with a few books and see how they work.

People say that you should not judge a book by its cover. If you are serious about making money by selling ebooks, you should understand that people do judge books by their cover, or at least having a beautiful cover can draw more attention to your book, which can increase sales. Make sure that every ebook that you sell has a beautiful book cover. If you do not know how to make your own cover, you might want to hire people from *Fiverr* to do the work for you. You can get your book cover for just $5 (per book).

Now, once you have your ebook ready and complete, then you now have a product that you can sell. A nice thing about an ebook is that it has unlimited supply without you having to spend anything. Once you have your ebook, then it is with you forever, and people can buy as many copies as they want. Hence, only the initial cost can be quite high (if you hire a ghostwriter), but then after that, you will have a product that you can sell as many times as you can at no cost on your part.

Okay, having a product is one thing, being able to sell it is another. Another important part of this business is marketing your ebook/s. There are many ways to do this. You can use social media, your blog, guest post on authority sites, and others. You should try to market your ebook as much as you can. Keep in mind that even if you have a wonderful product to sell, you cannot expect for it to generate profits if the market is not aware that your product even exists. You should promote your ebook. This is another reason why you should make sure that your ebook has a good quality. If you know that it has a bad quality, then you will have a hard time promoting it.

Quality is important. You simply cannot expect an ebook that has a poor quality to sell and generate a decent amount of profits. If you offer an ebook that has a bad quality, it will most likely end up with lots of negative reviews. In any kind of business, as well as when you are selling anything, quality is very important.

But, when it comes to an ebook, what exactly makes a work of high or at least good quality? Well, the book has to be able to satisfy the wants or needs of its readers. If it is a non-fiction book, then it has to provide the readers with useful information on the subject. It should also respect the basic rules on grammar and punctuation. It should relay the information in an easy to understand manner. It should also be properly formatted. Presentation is another important thing. Hence, it should have a catchy and interesting cover to draw more attention to the book, among other things. The more that you exert efforts to create a good book, the easier you will be able to sell it, and this means higher profits.

Making money by selling ebooks can be a highly rewarding venture. When you take this approach, you should learn to consider it as a business and not just a passion for writing and sharing your work. At present, the ebook industry is also competitive. Every day, new ebooks are being published. Still, it remains to be a lucrative business. You might have to publish several books before you can start to appreciate the flow of income. Although it is possible to have success with just one book, experts suggest that you can more effectively increase your sales by having more books for sale. You might want to try different genres and see which one works best for you. Another way that is recommended is to conduct your own research and analysis of the market and see the kind of books that sell. You can then write a book that relates to the latest trend. This way you will know that there is an existing market and demand for your ebook.

If you want to have a decent flow of passive income, then selling ebooks is definitely one of the best choices that you can make.

Instead of selling on Amazon and other online retailers, you also have an option to sell directly from your own website or blog. This way, you will enjoy full control of everything. It is also a good way to earn a higher income per sale. However, you will also be responsible for everything, such as in promoting your ebooks, processing payments, and others.

The key to Kindle publishing success is to produce high-quality books and publish as many books as you can. Both quality and quantity are important. You also need a strong marketing arm to be able to promote your products (ebooks) effectively. Indeed, many people have made a fortune by selling ebooks on Amazon and on other online bookstores. You might also want to use various pen names depending on the genre of your books. Of course, you are also free to use your real name if you want. Indeed, when it comes to making money online, selling ebooks is something that has been proven to be a good way to make lots of money.

➢ Blogging

Blogging is another popular way to earn money online. There are many blogs out there that earn thousands and even millions of dollars. What is a blog? Well, a blog is like a digital diary or journal that is shared with the world. Blogs are so famous that you can think of anything topic that you want and you will surely find related blogs out there somewhere just by doing a search online. It should be noted that the blog itself does not make money, but what you do with it can allow you to generate a nice income. A common way to earn money from your blog is through the use of ads. This is where ads will be posted on your blog, and you can earn every time a visitor clicks on the ads and/or per 1,000 views. There are many ad programs out there, but the one that is most recommended is Google AdSense. This is what professional bloggers use. And, since it is owned by Google, you can rest for sure that you can trust it. However, unlike other ad programs, it is not that easy to be qualified to be part of the Google AdSense programs. You first need to send an application to Google, and it should allow you to post Google ads on your blog. Although many bloggers have a hard time to get approved, it is worth noting that if you know the right steps, then you can easily be approved to post Google ads. Here are notable points that you should know:

- Regular traffic

Before you even send your application to Google, you should first establish regular traffic to your blog. It does not have to be a huge traffic, but you should at least have regular blog visitors. Hence, you will have to spend a few weeks or months working on your blog before you apply for Google AdSense. Getting regular traffic to your blog or site might be a real challenge in the beginning. But, just stick to the best practices, and you will soon establish your own traffic and a good following online.

- Contents

Your blog should already have some contents. Otherwise, Google will most likely not approve your application. There are no hard and fast rules as to how many posts you should have on your blog, but it is suggested that it should have at least 20 quality posts to have a good chance of being approved for the AdSense program.

Having contents on your blog will also help Google to identify what your blog is about. This is important to know the kind of ads that will be displayed on your blog.

- Quality

Last but not least, make sure that your blog has a good quality; otherwise, Google will definitely not approve your application. What you need is a good-quality blog. This means that your blog should be presentable and professional. It must also have decent contents and a good following. It does not have to be a perfect blog but at least make it presentable enough. Do not make it hard for Google to approve your blog. The more that you are able to establish your blog the higher is your chances of being approved by Google.

When it comes to blogging, one very important element that you should know is SEO. SEO stands for search engine optimization. This refers to how visible and discoverable your blog is on the Internet. Ideally, your blog should be on the first page of a search result. However, this can be quite challenging considering the level of competition and number of blogs in the market. With the help of SEO, you can increase your online visibility. This is important since no matter how amazing your blog is, you cannot expect for it to generate any decent traffic if it is hard to find online. Indeed, without the use of effective SEO, it is impossible to generate decent and regular traffic to your blog. Let us now discuss important SEO techniques that you should know:

➢ Long-tail keywords

When it comes to SEO, the number one thing that you should know is how to use keywords. Gone are the days when you can just use any keywords that you want. Today, you need to learn to use long-tail keywords. These keywords are composed of at least three targeted words to help increase the visibility of a particular blog post. Needless to say, it should be related to the blog post that you are promoting. For example, if you manage a business blog, do not just use the word *business* as your keywords. Instead, use long-tail keywords like *how to trade goods from Alaska* or any other related long-tail keywords. It also helps to make it specific. Also, remember that long-tail keywords should be composed of at least three words. Now, the next concern would be identifying the keywords that you should use. After all, there are countless of keywords that you can come up, so how do you know which keywords have a market? The way to do this is to use a keywords checker. Many bloggers recommend using Google Keyword Planner. With Google Keyword Planner, you will be able to tell how many times certain keywords or keyword phrase is searched for online. It will also give you suggestions of other keywords that you can use. To be able to access the Google Keyword Planner, you should have an AdWords account.

Google AdWords is a Google program that will allow you to post ads. This is different from AdSense where you allow other people to post ads on your blog. With AdSense, you are the one who is posting ads. Do not worry; you do not need to post ads. If you just want to use the Keywords Planner, then you can do so without having to pay for anything. Once you have an AdSense account, then you can have access to Google Keyword Planner. Picking the right keywords is important as it will significantly help you increase the blog's traffic. When it comes to any online business, getting good traffic is important as this allows you to get customers or buyers. Indeed, when it comes to SEO, the use of keywords tops the list.

➤ Keyword density

You also need to observe the right keyword density. What is keyword density? It simply refers to the number of times that your keywords are repeated in the article. Years ago, you can easily appear on the first page of search engines by repeating your chosen keywords many times. However, search engines have already developed and now ensure that those that appear on the first pages of the SERP (search engine results pages) have good quality. Hence, you cannot just fill your content with keywords. In fact, filling your content with keywords is now known as keyword stuffing which is not considered a good practice. When a search engine detects that you are involved in the practice of keyword stuffing, it will give your content a lower SEO ranking, which makes it less visible to search engines. As you can see, it is important that you observe the right keyword density to avoid search engines from thinking that you are engaged in keyword stuffing. So, what is the right keyword density? There is no strict rule on this matter yet. However, various expert bloggers agree that a good keyword density would be around 3%-5%. This refers to the number of times that your keywords should appear in your article.

You should also avoid the practice of forcing to repeat your keywords in an article. The keywords should flow smoothly in the article that your readers will barely notice that you even use keywords. Pay attention to the flow of the article. Take note that the use of keywords is only a part of your posting. The more important part is to provide quality information that your readers will enjoy and find helpful.

> Share

You have to share your content. Even if you come up with a good post, you cannot just rely on search engines to find and promote your content. It is your job to market and promote what you have posted. Do not worry; this is not difficult to do. A good and effective way to do this is by sharing your content on social media. When it comes to sharing, social media is your number one solution. However, you should take note that you must first have something that is worth sharing. You would not want to irritate your followers and connections with senseless and low-quality posts. So, once you have a content that you are proud of, something that you know that your target readers will find useful, then you can tap the power of social media to reach a bigger market.

One of the best things about social media is that those who like your content can share it with their own network. Do you realize its potential? This means that every time a person shares your content, you get to tap with a new set of network. Now, just imagine what will happen if many of these people like and share your content. This is actually how a content gets viral online. But, of course, for this to happen, you should ensure that you have something that is worth sharing. Make sure that every post that you make gives value to your readers. Once again, quality has to be your number one priority.

Indeed, when you engage in blogging, SEO is one thing that you should focus on. With high-quality contents and the right SEO strategy, you can be a successful blogger.

Blogging is definitely one of the best and is the most popular way to make money online. It is also a way to establish your expertise on a particular subject, provided that you are able to post useful information. Even today, some people earn a full-time income working as a blogger.

➢ Affiliate marketing

Another way to earn money online is through affiliate marketing. What is affiliate marketing? It is where you sell the products of other people. You then earn a share (income) every time a person purchases the product that you promote. When you work as an affiliate, you will be given an *affiliate link*. This is the link that you give to your readers. They can buy the product that you promote through this link. When a person buys a product through this link, then you will get your cut or share from the sale. This is how you earn money as an affiliate. Now, there are also programs that will reward you with a small fee every time your affiliate link gets clicked even if a sale is not consummated. Still, if you want to earn a decent income by being an affiliate marketer, your aim is to make your readers buy the product that you promote via your affiliate link.

If you want to be a successful affiliate marketer, then you need to establish your presence online. It is strongly advised that you put up a nice blog. Now, a common mistake is to oversell a product. Although your objective is to be able to sell something, you should know that overselling a product can be bad for your reputation. One thing that you should focus on is building trust with your readers. Take note that it is hard, if not impossible, to build trust when the readers know that you will make money from them. Gone are the days when you can just promote something and expect for people to be fooled easily and click on your affiliate link. When you work as an affiliate marketer, you need to work on establishing trust. After all, you cannot expect a person to buy from your link if he does not even trust you.

So, how can you gain the trust of your readers? Well, you need to give them value. This means that you should tell them the truth. Never lie to your readers. If there is something bad about a particular product, then be open and honest about it. Your readers will appreciate it if you are honest. After all, people do not expect for any product to be completely perfect. In fact, if you do not know any negative thing about a particular product, then chances are that you probably do not know it that much yet.

By doing a simple search online, you will find lots of affiliate programs. You can choose whether you want to use multiple affiliate programs or simply focus on a single program. One of the most successful affiliate programs is *Clickbank*.

It is up to you if you want to promote a particular product. Just avoid making it look like you just want to be able to sell the product. You should consider that your readers want to know the pros and cons of buying a product. He does not read your content to be encouraged to buy something. Instead, he is being careful. Do not make him buy something that you know will only make him disappointed. Doing so will only make you lose your customers.

You might want to come up with a review website. You can also make an honest comparison of competing products. The important thing is to give valuable information to your readers.

So, just how much can you make? Well, many successful affiliate marketers earn thousands of dollars every month. There are those who work as an affiliate marketer on a full-time basis. Unfortunately, if you do not give it enough focus and efforts, you might end up like other affiliate marketers who barely make any income. But, do not worry; with the right approach and hard work, you can make your affiliate marketing experience a pleasant and fruitful one. It just really takes time to establish yourself as an affiliate marketer, especially in the beginning. Just persist, and you will soon be able to reap the fruits of your labor.

It is also advised that you establish your online presence in social media. Successful affiliate marketers know how effective social media is. When it comes to gaining traffic and exposure, then the power of social media can be harnessed.

You might want to focus on a particular niche, but you can also come up with a site that reviews various products. It is recommended that you review products that you understand. For example, if you are personally interested and knowledgeable in computers, then you might want to write blog posts about various computer products. You can also make comparisons of the latest models from different brands. Of course, this is just an example. There is actually no limit on how you want to approach affiliate marketing.

Since you will earn a particular percentage from every sale, it means that a product that has a higher price will most likely give you a higher profit. However, this does not mean that there is no money for products that have a low price. When you market a product that has a low price, the key is to make sales by the volume. It is easy for people to buy cheap products, but they tend to be more careful before they purchase expensive products.

So, is it for you? If you are fond of making product reviews, then you might enjoy working as an affiliate marketer. It is worth repeating that to be successful, you need to establish trust. To do this, you should provide your audience with true and helpful information regarding the product that you are marketing.

There are many other ways to earn money online. This is because the online world connects you with people, and these people can be your customers/clients. Indeed, if you want to increase your income, you should definitely look into putting up your own online business. Another advantage of running an online business is that it allows you to connect to a big market. When you have an online presence, the whole world becomes your potential market. It is just a matter of pulling the right strings and positioning yourself properly. Although it may take some time to establish your presence online, it is nonetheless doable and is very much worth it.

Step 3 — Learn a High Income Producing Skill

If your income is still not enough, or if you simply want to further increase your earning capacity so you can quickly achieve your objective of having 6 months of savings, then you should learn a high income producing skill. This way, you can have a higher income per month. Although it is true that you can make money regardless of the kind of work that you do, it is also true that there are certain work or work positions that simply get a much higher pay than others. However, such positions usually require technical knowledge. The good news is that you do not have to enroll in a formal class just to learn them. You can learn these skills by reading from books or even just by doing a diligent research online. Let us take a look at some of these key work positions that can significantly give your income a boost:

- Digital marketing: PPC manager, social media marketing, web design

All these deal with the online world. Indeed, digital marketing is very important for businesses these days. If a business does not have an online presence, then you can expect that it is probably far behind the competition. If you can learn digital marketing, then there is a demand for what you can do. You do not have to learn the whole aspect of digital marketing. If you want, you can just specialize on a particular subject. For example, as a PPC manager, you will have to deal with advertisements. PPC stands for *pay per click*. It is where you buy visits to your site or blog by posting ads online instead of merely relying on search engines to find and display your site. As a PPC manager, you will have to run and monitor ads and make sure that the ads are able to promote the site or blog effectively. You need to be able to target your market properly to increase your chances of turning visitors into actual conversions (sales, sign-ups, or whatever your objective might be). You also need to be able to write short yet compelling ads, among others. Indeed, the job of a PPC marketer is also quite challenging, but it is nonetheless learnable. If you give it enough time and effort, you will surely be able to master the ins and outs of PPC advertising, and businesses will definitely want to work with you.

Social media marketing is another very hot service today. If you can promote something online effectively, then many businesses and people would want to work with you. Considering how helpful and important social media is, people spend money just to establish their presence online. But, of course, to be able to market something effectively through social media, you need to have a strong presence and quality following first. The good news is that once you have established yourself, then there are a lot of things that you can do, and this opens the gate to opportunities to make a nice profit.

- Web design

The design of one's site or blog can make a difference. Many times, the design alone separates professional blogs and sites from unprofessional ones. If you learn web design and get good at it, you can charge a premium price for your services. Indeed, many businesses pay a high price just to have someone to design their website. If you have an eye for the right designs and combination of colors, then this is probably the job for you. Professional web designers normally charge thousands of dollars per project. This is also something that you can do on the side while you keep your regular job.

Having a professionally-designed blog or site is important to any business. If a particular site is poorly designed, then chances are that people will also not take it seriously. If people do not treat you seriously, then you cannot expect to earn any decent income. As a web designer, you are going to help people and businesses attract their market with your catchy and grabbing web designs. If you ever take this approach, prepare to learn some computer coding.

- Programming

Since we live in the age of computers and the Internet, it is clear that programming is considered to be highly essential. There is simply a high demand for programmers. After all, everything that happens and exists online depends on programming. If you know how to program properly, then you are a key asset in any online business. The good news is that you do not need to take any formal study to be a good programmer. There are many books, including free books online, that will teach you how to program effectively. Although programming can be considered a highly technical field, it is also something where you can earn a high pay. Again, there is a huge demand for programmers. The truth is that every blog or site requires application of programming. Hence, not only will you be able to earn a good income as a programmer, but you are assured that there will always be a continuing demand for your services.

There are also many videos on YouTube that will teach you the basics of programming. If you are not that knowledgeable when it comes to computers, you might find it very challenging to understand even the basic codes. However, do not be discouraged. Coding is actually simpler than you might think. If you give it enough time and effort, you can be a good programmer.

- High-Ticket Sales

This is about selling expensive products online, usually belonging to other people like businesses. This works just like affiliate marketing but can be more challenging in the sense that people tend to be more careful with spending their money when it comes to expensive things. However, despite the challenge, this can be a highly lucrative career where you can earn lots of money even from a single transaction. There are people out there who make a living and earn lots of money solely from high-ticket sales.

When you take this route, you definitely need to establish a good rapport with your customers. Hence, you need to establish trust. Needless to say, the way to do this is to give value. If you want to focus on high-ticket sales, it is strongly advised that you put up a professional blog. This is the way for you to gain the trust of your audience. Some people try to be successful simply by focusing on social media, but it is not considered the best approach. Of course, social media is still important, especially in terms of sharing your work and reaching a bigger market, but the way to connect with your potential buyers and be able to earn their trust is by putting up your own blog or site and posting helpful contents.

It is also worth noting that high-ticket sales should not just be about making a successful sale. Just like with affiliate marketing, you need to focus more on building a good relationship with people. You need to earn their trust. This is the way to have a continuous business. You would not want to gamble and lose everything just for one sale. As long as you stick to the right practices and are able to build a good relationship, then sales will follow on their own. But, if you become too greedy and be concerned with how you can earn money than helping people by providing useful information, then it would be difficult even to consummate a single high-ticket sale.

- Freelance writing

When it comes to making money online, freelance writing is always on the list. In fact, majority of the people who earn money online are related to freelance writing. This is easy to understand since every website or blog needs contents. Not to mention, blogs need a continuous supply of fresh contents to keep it active. So, if you want to earn nice income online, then you should definitely try freelance writing online.

So, how much do freelance writers make? Well, the price varies. Those who are just starting out and are still learning how to write earn a few dollars per article, but if you get good at it, you can earn hundreds of dollars for a single article.

Beginning freelance writers normally start with content mills like Upwork or Freelancer. However, if you want to earn a good amount of income, it should be noted that going to content mills is not your best option. They are only good if you just want to practice writing but not to earn a good income. However, as an exception, you might find good-paying clients from content mills although the chances are slim. If you want to earn a decent amount of income by freelance writing, you should send your work directly to publishers that pay for freelance work. There are many sites, and blogs out there that accept pitches and works from freelance and they would pay you for accepted pieces. If you freelance to authority sites, you can earn a decent amount per article. If you write for content mills, the usual rate is just a poor $3 per 500-word article. You can compare that to writing for established sites that pay on average at least $60 per article, and the price can go even much higher. So, if you think you have a good way with words or if you are willing to give yourself through time and practice, then you can definitely earn a nice income by freelance writing alone. In fact, there are people out there who earn a living solely through freelance writing.

There is a huge demand for people who can write high-quality articles. Businesses are also willing to pay a premium price for excellent writers. However, it should be noted that writing is a skill and an art. You cannot just expect for your work to be accepted for publication if you do not know how to write effectively. However, do not be disheartened; the truth is that writing can be learned. As long as you are willing to give it enough time to practice and study it, then you can significantly improve your writing over time.

When you work as a freelance writer, you need to learn how to write pitches. A pitch is a letter that is normally directed to an editor where you pitch a story (article) that you will provide. Take note that this is not just about telling the editor what you want to write, but you should also show why it is a good piece for the publishing house, as well as why you are the right person to write it.

However, before you write your pitch letter, there are certain things that you need to take note of. The first thing that you want to know is if the website or blog accepts pitches or works from freelance writers. Normally, you'll know about this by checking the editorial section of the site, if any. If there are none, you can simply send a message via the site's *Contact Us* page. Once your pitch letter is accepted, the editor will tell you if you can commence with writing the article. You may have to prepare to do some revisions. Normally, you will be paid after your work is finally accepted for publication.

As a freelance writer, you can write to multiple publishers. In fact, this is actually how freelance writers normally make money. The more sites and blogs that you write for, the higher potential income will be. It is also not unusual for a freelance writer to get some sort of regular work from a client. This happens when a client is happy with your work. Hence, it is always important to focus on the quality of your work.

Indeed, freelance writing can be a highly lucrative career. There are people out there who are able to leave their day job and just freelance full time in the comfort of their homes without a boss to please. But, of course, this does not mean that you will have fewer responsibilities. Although you have no boss to please, you will now have clients and editors to work with. Being your own boss also means being responsible for everything. If you stop writing from too long, then the flow of income will also stop. This is one of the challenges faced by freelance writers. However, if you are personally fond of writing, then you may find this path to be very rewarding and highly enjoyable.

- Ghostwriting

This is another branch of freelance writing. However, unlike freelance writing where you normally keep the byline, you will not receive any credit when you work as a ghostwriter. As a ghostwriter, you write something for a client and not earn any credit for the work. You will only be paid for your work, but you will not claim any ownership over the work. It is the client who owns your work. It is noteworthy to that majority of published books are made by ghostwriters. Since you will not claim any ownership or credit over the work, you can charge a much higher fee than doing a typical freelance writing job. Professional ghostwriters earn more than $10,000 per book. In fact, it is not unusual for professional ghostwriters to charge more than $20,000 per book. Indeed, working as a ghostwriter can be a highly lucrative career. There are also simple and small-time ghostwriting projects that you can take where you can earn a few hundred dollars for writing a short book. This is not bad at all especially if you just want to earn something to pay the bills or simply to practice your writing skills, as well as while you are waiting for a big project to come. Some freelance writers end up working as a full-time ghostwriter. The term ghostwriter is usually associated with ghostwriting books, but it is worth noting that ghostwriting is not limited to writing books. As a ghostwriter, you can also ghostwrite articles, blog posts, brochures and manuals, poems, and even song lyrics. It is all about doing something where someone else is going to take the credit for your work. For this reason, ghostwriters are able to charge a much higher amount than the usual.

Another interesting thing about working as a ghostwriter is the upfront fees. When you work as a book ghostwriter, you can ask your client for an upfront fee which can be as high as 50% or even 60% (or even higher) of the total price. This is something that you will discuss and negotiate with your client. This is normal in ghostwriting. After all, you will be writing a book, and it will most likely take time for you to finish it. Hence, it is just right to ask for an upfront fee. The said fee can also act as some form of acceptance fee, as well as for your security as you work on the project. After all, it would be an unlikely situation to start working carefully on a client's book without being sure if the client would even pay you.

There are professional ghostwriters out there who make a fine living just by ghostwriting books. If you enjoy writing books, then this is definitely something that you should consider. Just remember that when you work as a ghostwriter, you do not get any credit for your work. Your work belongs to your client as if the client was the one who wrote it.

Step 4 — Get a Freelance or Part-Time Job Using Your New Skill

Now that you have a new skill whether from your current work or on your own, you can now use it to make more money. The way to do this is to get a part-time freelance job using your new skill. This is definitely an effective way to supplement your income and make more money. Every new skill can be used for something where you can get paid. What people often overlook is that there is something that they can do to make a nice profit. Now, once you know you are ready to offer your skill to others, it is time to make people know about it. You cannot expect for work to appear just out of nowhere. You need to market your expertise; otherwise, you will have trouble with finding any clients.

So, how do you promote your service? Again, the best way to do this is to have a website or a blog, you can then use the power of social media to help spread the word about what you do. The more people you reach through your site and social media promotions, the higher is your chance to get clients. Since you will not be quitting your day job, you should make it clear that you will only render freelance work part-time. When you are just starting out, it is not really advised that you quit your day job right away. Freelancing is like a business. You cannot expect to make profits from it right away. It will also take time to establish yourself in the market. So, to be safe, do not quit your usual job and jump into freelancing full time right away. You need to be careful with your decisions, especially if there are people who depend on you for support. Do not worry; the important thing is that there is progress and that you are moving forward.

- Improve your skills and create connections in the industry

You cannot just be content with your present skills. Continuous improvement has to be a constant priority. It does not matter whether you work as a marketer, a writer, programmer, or whatever position you take, there is always something that you can do to be better. You should not overlook the existing competition between and among freelancers. These days, many people are turning to freelance jobs, so you should definitely give this and its implications some considerations, especially with respect to how it can affect your business.

Another thing that you can do is to improve your connections in the industry that you engage in. By building useful connections, you can have more flow of work, and this means more income. Who knows, you might even reach the point where you can totally leave your day job and work as a freelancer full time. This way, you can have more control over your time and your life.

A good way to build connections is by using LinkedIn. LinkedIn is a social media platform just like Facebook. However, the key difference is that LinkedIn is a social media platform specially made for professionals. This is where you can get key contacts of people who might be related to your business and could help you with your business. However, do not forget that it is still just a social media platform; hence, do not expect so much from it. It is still you who needs to do the hard work. Still, if used effectively, you can tap this social media channel to propel your business by connecting with the right people.

It is also good to use LinkedIn to allow you to meet and connect with influencers. Influencers are people who are considered as experts in their field of knowledge, and they often have a quality following. Take note that this refers to quality following and not just the number of followers or connections that an influencer has. Quality connections refer to people who would actually engage in what you share. Unfortunately, there are also people who simply ignore what their connections share with them. So, why do you want to connect with an influencer? Well, just imagine what can happen if an influencer supports and promotes your posts? You can effectively draw a huge market, which means more clients or customers. So, how do you make an influencer promote your work? Well, the number one thing that you need is to have something that is worthy of being promoted, something that an influencer would also find interesting and helpful. Now, you can simply connect with an influencer of LinkedIn by sending him/her a connection request. If it gets accepted, then you will be finally connected. In which case, you can now send him a direct message. This is where you will get to communicate directly with an influencer and maybe ask him to help you. Of course, an influencer is not obliged to support you. The best way to convince an influencer to help you is by making him see that you are also valuable. The best way to do this is to provide useful and interesting contents. If an influencer sees that you are really serious about what you do and that you are good at it, then he will most likely respond to your messages and even work with you. Take note that it is also not uncommon for an influencer to charge you for helping promote you online.

Of course, LinkedIn is not the only way to establish more connections. You can also use and distribute business cards. You can also make use of email signatures to help promote your business. You can even use the usual social media channel like Facebook to establish more connections. The important thing is to make people know about what you offer and be able to establish a connection with them.

Another network that you should establish comes from referrals from your own clients. In fact, this one is very important. Through referrals alone, there is a chance that you can have a well-established business. This is another reason why you should ensure that you render work of high quality. Your clients cannot refer you to another if they are not satisfied with your work. Hence, the quality of your work should always be your main priority. You should also keep your clients on your contact list. It is also advised that you message them every now and then even just to ask how they are doing. This is how you maintain a good relationship. Do not be discouraged if a client could not hire or give you more work today, you may not know when you might need him in the future.

It should also be noted that there is no end to improving one's skills. If you think that you have already learned everything that is to know about a particular job position, then try to compare yourself with your competitors in the industry and identify your strengths and weaknesses. Take note that your strengths and weaknesses are relative to the strengths and weaknesses of your competitors. You can also branch out and learn other related skills. The important thing is to always keep on making progress and improvements. Improving one's skill is a never-ending journey. This is also why it is advised that you just enjoy the learning process and do not rush it. It will not end anyway, so there is nothing much for you to worry about. The important thing is to keep on learning and improving.

- Increase your income and build confidence

As you continue to engage in this kind of work, you will learn ways to further increase your income. Also, as you get more projects done, you will have more confidence in yourself. This will come over time as you get used to your acquired skill.

At the beginning of your career, you might not have enough confidence in yourself. This is because you are still unaware of what you can do. This is true, especially if you know that you still have not mastered the skill involved in the service that you offer. However, as you gain more experience, you will also gain more confidence. This is also the skill and confidence that you need to be able to take on bigger projects.

When you are just starting out, you might be tempted to hit a big project right away. Although this can be an opportunity to make big money, you should be sure that you can handle the task properly. If the skill required is something that you are not that confident in, then you might want to start out with small yet decent projects. This is a good way to gain more experience and confidence in what you can do.

As you gain more confidence and as you further develop your skill, you can start to charge higher rates. Of course, this means that you should also target the right market – those who can pay.

Something that you should realize is that opportunities come from other people. Hence, if you want to have more opportunities to earn money like getting new projects with a higher pay, then you need to reach out and connect with the right people. Now, when it comes to connecting to people, many would advise the use of social media. However, you should not overlook the reach of your own blog or website. If you set it up properly with the right SEO techniques, then you will also have your own network from your site. This network will most probably be composed of people who are interested in the service that you offer.

It is possible for you to grow your income significantly to the point that you will feel as if you could leave your job and just work full time as a freelancer. In fact, this is how people become full-time freelancers. In the beginning, they think that it is just a way to supplement their income until they realize that they could earn so much more money if they work as a full-time freelancer. Normally, this happens once you have established a good client base that you are assured a regular flow of projects.

Should you work as a full-time freelancer?

If your freelance business succeeds, you will definitely reach a point where you will be asking yourself if you should just leave your office work and just work as a full-time time freelancer as you try to reach your objective of getting enough savings for 6 months. Well, this is something that you need to decide on carefully. You need to weigh the consequences of leaving your job. Is your freelancing business enough to support itself? Do you get a consistent flow of freelance projects? How long do you think will you be able to maintain it? Think about and analyze every detail to be sure of your decision. Indeed, leaving your secured 9-5 job and becoming a full-time freelancer can be a life-changing experience that you need to consider carefully. This is something that only you can answer. The important thing is to be completely honest with yourself as you come up with a firm decision.

If you can reach your objective without leaving your secured 9-5 job, then perhaps it is safer for you to just be more patient until you achieve your objective. This way, you are sure that you do not have to take any risks. However, if you are more of the adventurous type and if you think that your freelance business can now support itself, then you might want to become a full-time freelancer.

If you feel the freelance business is also the dream job that you have always wanted, then that is really good for you. However, you can also do freelancing just for the sake of increasing your income, which is not a bad thing. After all, there is an objective that you need to accomplish, and being able to raise enough savings to support you and your family for 6 months is not a joke. In fact, it might take you more than a year to do it. This is why you have to exert all efforts to be able to do it as quickly as possible.

Continuity of business is important. If your freelance or online business will only give you a decent income for a few months only, then it is not safe to quit your regular job. Just like any other business, an online business or a freelance business has to be well established. While you are still setting it up, you cannot rely on it completely. If you have a family to support and a mortgage to worry about, you definitely would not want to take too much risk.

You have to be objective when it comes to analyzing your business. Pay attention to how much it actually makes than how much you think it could make. Although it is good to exercise positive thinking, you should still learn to recognize the hard facts and problems that you might be facing. To be safe, it might be the best option for you not to quit your job even if you are confident that your freelance or online business would be enough to support your needs. The key is to quit your job only when you are certain that what you have now is enough. There are two things that you need: a 6-month savings and a side income that also makes good money. Take note that although it is referred to as a side income, it does not mean that it does not earn well. It should, if possible, be as good or nearly as good as your current income source.

You do not always have to manage an online business or a freelance business. You also have a choice to just apply to another company or simply get another work other than your normal 9-5 work. Just do not make it too hard. Remember that you will only need it to supplement your current income. Hence, if you are really not into the use of computers, then you might want to take other kinds of work relevant to your skill. For example, if your current job relates to health and nutrition, you might want to work as a freelance nutritionist and recommend food and diet programs to people who want to become fit and healthy. Of course, this is just an example. The possibilities are endless and would depend on your learned skill or any skill that you are willing to learn.

Promote your freelance or online business

No matter how good you are, it will be a challenge to have clients or customers if the market is not even aware that you exist. You should understand that the online world is a big world out there. Although you have the potential to reach a big market, the level of competition is also tight. Other people offer the same services as you do. These people are also putting in time, money, and effort to promote their services. However, you do not have to directly compete with them. The important thing is for you to do something to make the market know that your business exists and that you are ready and able to offer them your services. So, how can you effectively spread the word about your services? Here are notable things that you should do:

- Call to action

Make sure that your blog posts make use of a call to action. What is a call to action? As the name implies, it is about telling your readers what to do. This is usually added at the end of an article. For example, you can write something like this: *If you are looking for a _____, then click here.* You can then lead your readers to a page where you offer your products or services. This way, you first give your audience some useful information which helps build trust. After that, you get to offer them your services. As you can see, it is important that you provide your readers with helpful contents; otherwise, they will probably not consider hiring your services or buying your products, as the case may be.

A call to action has to be short yet direct. Limit it to just one or two short sentences. The important thing is to direct the readers to what you want them to read next. Do not make it seem as if you were trying to deceive your readers. Instead, you should make it look natural as if you are just helping or guiding your readers. This is not a form of manipulation but should be more like offering help to the readers through your services.

- Improve your SEO

By writing contents optimized for SEO, you can increase your site's/blog's visibility online. Take note that every new visitor that you lead to your site is a potential customer. The more that you improve your SEO ranking, the more people will find your site. Hence, make sure to observe the best SEO practices with every post that you make.

- Share on social media

Of course, when it comes to making a noise and informing people about something, social media tops the list. This is why you need to work on having a strong and quality following on social media. Now, the problem is when you have just started to use social media or you simply do not have any good following. In this case, you can start building a strong network of connections now. A good way to do this quickly is to look for someone who is active and already has a strong following on the niche or subject related to your business. Try to establish a good connection with this person by writing comments or sharing his works. If you do this to several people, chances are that some of them would also share your work, and this is a good way to tap a big market and gain more followers. Of course, to increase the chances of success, you need to make sure that you provide high-quality contents.

Now, when you share or promote your business on social media, you need to observe some ethical rules. You should not bombard your connections with lots of posts. As a rule, only promote your own stuff around 3-5 times a day. You should also learn to support and promote others. Take note that when you use social media, you should also learn to focus on other people. If you want others to give you any attention, then you should also give them attention.

You should also not post a full article. Instead, just write a good short introduction to hook a reader, and then provide a link to your blog or website. You should also include a picture. According to research, you can get more clicks if also include a picture to your posting. Needless to say, the image should be relevant to your article.

- Support group

There is nothing wrong with asking for some support from your family and friends. This can be very helpful, especially when you are just starting out. If you have a friend who is active and has a good following on social media, then that is a big plus. You do not have to beg people to help promote your site. If you are not comfortable asking for help, then simply let them know that you have a website or blog. Out of goodwill, it is up to them if they would like to help you promote it. This is an effective way to get followers quickly.

- AdWords

Perhaps one of the best ways to promote your online or freelance business especially when you are just starting out is to use AdWords. AdWords is a Google program that will allow you to promote your site or blog by displaying Google ads on search engines and other pages. This is a paid service, but it is very much worth it. Unlike other ad programs, you will only be charged when somebody actually clicks on your advertisement. If your ads are only viewed and not clicked, then you do not have to pay anything. Hence, you truly get your money's worth. You only pay when a person actually sees your page. You also have the option to choose any part of your blog or site where you will lead your audience. If you are just starting out and still have some issues with gaining visibility online and withdrawing traffic to your blog, then Google AdWords can be very helpful. And, since it is owned by the Internet giant, Google, you know that you can rely on it.

Another interesting feature of using AdSense is that you can use targeted keywords. This means that your ads will only appear when certain keywords are searched for in the search box. You can also target the countries and even specific cities where you want your ads to appear. Thus, if you just want your ads to appear in the US or any particular city or cities therein, then you can do that as well. The cost is also very much reasonable. You can adjust and specify just how much you are willing to spend per click.

When you use AdWords, you will also be the one who will design the advertisement that will appear. The key is to make your advertisement short, direct, and catchy. Also, make sure that you have a good page where you direct your audience after they click on your ad. If you are selling a product, say, an ebook, then you can direct them to your sales page.

- Specialized page/ Sales page

This is probably the most important part of a blog room website. This is where you feature your product or service and convince people to hire or buy from you. Here, you will highlight your product/service and make your offer. Of course, you do not have to make it obvious that you want to make a sale or be hired. Rather, a person who visits this page should feel and know that he needs to hire you. Or, in case you are selling something, that he would want to buy it. Instead of telling people to buy your product, you should let them know why they would want to buy what you offer. This page should identify a problem and a solution to that problem. Of course, the solution to that problem would be whatever it is that you offer.

You might also want to read on copywriting or even hire a professional copywriter to write your sales page.

Step 5 — Quit Your Job

Okay, so here is the last step. Unlike the previous one, you should now be sure that you can support yourself and your family even if you let go of your present job. By this time, you should already have your 6 months of savings, as well as a profitable side income, which could be your online or freelance business. Since you have enough savings for 6 months, the side income does not need to generate such money to cover for all of your bills. But, of course, you should make it as profitable as possible. After all, this is the part where you will embark upon a new path in your life. It is also worth noting that this is not saying goodbye to work. Rather, this is more about living the life that you want, which includes having the work that you have always wanted. Hence, you will still make money in the process. However, you simply cannot expect the transition to happen quickly, so it is best to have some money in reserve.

Okay, so this step is more concerned about quitting your job. This is where you ask yourself if you can now safely quit your job. How much savings do you have? Will you be able to support yourself for 6 months without any problem? Are you sure that you want to leave your secured 9-5 job?

Once you reach this step, it is not unusual to suddenly feel confused or uncertain; however, this is a decision that you need to make. You need to be objective about this. You should honestly assess the situation. There are two opposing forces that you should be careful with. The first one is fear. Fear is where you can now quit your job and live the life that you have always wanted, but since you are full of fear, you deprive yourself from having this chance. This is where you cling to your secured 9-5 job even though you know that it does not give you fulfillment or happiness. Fear can prevent you from taking the next step and making positive changes. Remember that in life you need to take risks. This is how you can grow and develop. If you do not take risks, then you will always be stuck in the routine that you want to escape from.

The next hindrance to your success would be the opposite of fear, and that is being too arrogant to the point that you fail to recognize your weaknesses. The problem here is that you do not make the necessary changes or adjustments. So, if you realize that what you have is not enough to support you and your family from 6 months and that your side income is also not enough to provide your needs, then do not quit your job right away. Do not make big assumptions that you will soon be successful. You have to consider your obligations and be sure that you will be able to meet all of your obligations.

Instead of submitting to fear or arrogance, you should be more careful by taking the right approach and being more confident. Confidence comes from knowledge and being assured of your capabilities. When assessing your situation, you should be honest and face all of the facts of the situation.

It is noteworthy that finally quitting your job is a very serious decision that will surely have an impact on your life, so this is definitely something that you have to consider seriously. You should realize that if you do not quit your job, then you will forever be trapped in your current routine. This means that you might never be able to live the life that you have always wanted.

Take the step – only once you have 6 months savings and if you have a side income that replaces your main income

Once you are sure that you are ready, when you know that you have enough savings for 6 months and that you also have a profitable side income that you can rely on, then it is time for you to take the step.

This is it! This is what you have worked for all this time. This is the moment when you finally leave your job and jump into the life that you have always dreamed of.

Whatever you want to do, then now is the time to do it. However, you should not forget about your responsibilities. Also, keep in mind that you still have to manage your online or freelance business even just as a side income as you work on whatever it is that you want to do.

If what you what to do is the online or freelance business that you have, then now is the time to go all in and work on it full time.

Taking this step is a very serious matter, but this is also what you have prepared for all this time. Finally, you can now live the life that you have always wanted. You are now in the position where you can take risks since you have enough buffer zone or margin for error. Of course, it was not easy to reach this stage, so make the most out of what you have. If your side income or business also happens to be your dream work, then you are in the perfect position. Still, either way, it is now just a matter of doing your best and experiencing the life that you have always wanted.

Now, many people, when they reach this point, they become afraid. This is true, especially when you are already used and have grown dependent on your 9-5 job, and this is understandable. After all, your current setup has already allowed you to gain 6 months of savings, which means that you are already doing well, so why take a sudden change? Another problem here is that it might be difficult for you to go back to your job after you quit. When thinking about the situation this way, the most logical reason would be for you to just remain as you are. However, you need to understand that doing so will not get you anywhere. If you limit yourself now and do not take risks, then you will never have the chance to live the life that you have always wanted. You have to understand that for you to live your dream life, then you need to take risks and sacrifices. As the saying goes, you cannot discover a new island without losing sight of the shore.

If you are afraid that you might not be able to return to your current work after you quit, you might want to take the time to talk with your boss about it. There is a good chance that he will be able to understand your situation. In fact, he might even encourage you to pursue your dream and give you some pieces of advice. Since you have reached this point, the recommended thing to do would be to pursue what you have always wanted.

So, this is it. Finally you can transition to the life that you want. You deserve it. You do not have to look back, but you have all the reasons and inspiration to look forward. With 6 months of savings and a profitable side income, you can now afford to take risks without any worry. This is why the preparation was also quite intense. After all, building six months of savings is not a joke. This is because, by the time you reach this point, you can finally put all your focus on whatever it is that you have always wanted without any worry. Make sure to do your best.

You might want to give yourself about two or three days to take a relaxing break before you fully transition to the kind of life that you want. If you do, use that time to relax and prepare yourself for a new journey that is to come. This is the best time for you to make your own reflections. Learn from your past and have a positive attitude towards the journey that is ahead of you. It is worth noting that this is not the end of your journey or work. In fact, this is only the beginning of a life that you have always dreamed of. Now, it is time for you to live that life and be successful. Do not think that there will be no challenges. No matter what path you take, especially if it is a meaningful one, then you should always expect challenges. These challenges will reveal your strengths and weaknesses, and they will make you grow as a person. Do not run away from challenges. Instead, face them with courage. Keep in mind that every mountain has its own risks and obstacles. If it is too easy to climb, then perhaps it is not worth climbing.

For now, this is your moment. You should make the best out of it. Finally, it is time for you to live the life that you have always wanted. Do not be afraid. Believe in yourself and make it count.

Best Practices

To increase your chances of success, you also need to learn certain best practices. These practices will ensure that you are able to execute the lessons in this book effectively. Let us discuss them one by one:

- Research

If you have a blog or site where you provide your audience with quality information, then be sure to do thorough research. Make sure that you give them facts and reliable information. This is how you build trust. As you already know by now, building trust is a very important element of your success. You do this by providing your readers with helpful information. To ensure that you give them the kind of information that your readers need, you have to do research. Now, many people do their research but fail to do sufficient research. There are no hard and fast rules as to what constitutes sufficient research. However, you can tell if the amount of research you have made is enough when you are confident and could justify everything that you have written. Needless to say, you should also cite your sources to avoid plagiarism issues. As much as possible, only cite from reputable sources. Even when you are engaged in the businesses of selling other people's products or affiliate marketing, it is your job to provide your audience with honest and useful information. Again, doing thorough research is the key to doing this. Make sure that every post that you make is backed up by a solid research. Never make assumptions, unless you make it clear to your readers that you are just making a reasonable assumption. Do your research at all times to provide high-quality information.

- Do not overthink

A common mistake is to keep on thinking when you are already in the process of execution. Of course, this does not mean that you should no longer think and reconsider what you are doing; however, you should avoid overthinking. A good way to do this is to have a plan. A plan should be made prior to execution. Once you start working on a plan, then make sure that you spend most of your time taking positive actions instead of overthinking. You are free to give yourself some time each day to think and reconsider your decision, but be sure to limit the time that you spend doing it. You do not want your focus to be divided. This is another reason why you should not rush with coming up with a plan. Once you have a plan, then know that it is time for you to execute it. You can still change your original plan if you realize that it is for the best after a careful consideration of the circumstances.

- Use links (inbound and outbound links)

Learn to incorporate links in your articles. A link acts as a call to action that directs a reader what to do next. An easy and effective way of doing this is by using a hyperlink. You can add a hyperlink to a particular phrase in your article that will lead the reader to another page, which could be a page in your blog or outside of your blog. If you direct your readers to another page within your blog, then that is referred to as an inbound link. If you refer your reader to a page outside of your blog, then that is referred to as an outbound link. You can use an outbound link whenever you cite a source. You can use an inbound link to direct your reader to another relevant article in your blog. This is a good way to make your articles promote themselves. However, avoid using too many links in an article. As a general rule, you can limit the use of links to just around 2 or 3 per article, depending on its length. Of course, the longer an article is, the more links you can use. Just avoid making it look like being bombarded with links.

- Offer a freebie

People love free stuff. The good thing is that when a person likes something that they got from you from freelance, the more they will be interested in your work. A good way to do this is to give them a free ebook on your site. This is how so many bloggers draw more followers. But, of course, before you can expect for anyone to think about downloading your ebook, you should make sure that your blog or site is already filled with useful information. The articles on your site are also something that you offer for free. The more that people like your blog posts, the more likely that they will want to download your free ebook.

- Grow your email list

It does not matter what kind of business or service that you offer. It is always important to focus on growing your email list. What is an email list? It is a list of subscribers to your blog or website. You are probably familiar with the *subscriber's* button that appears on most blogs. When a person subscribes to your blog, you can send him an email at any time. Subscribers will also be notified every time you make a new post on your blog. A good way to make people subscribe to your mailing list is by offering them a free ebook in exchange. After all, they are free to unsubscribe at any time.

- Respond to comments

If you manage a blog, be sure to respond to comments. This is a good way to establish a connection with your followers or readers. It does not matter whether you received one or even a hundred comments. As much as possible, you should respond to every comment. This is common ethics in the online world. You have to appreciate that the person has taken the time to write a comment, so it is only right and just that you give an appropriate response. This is a good way to build a good relationship with a reader. Take as much time as you need. The important thing is to make every person know that you are giving him attention. A simple "Thank you." would be enough, if you cannot say anything else.

Now, there are primarily two kinds of comments that you will receive: positive and negative. Of course, there is no problem when you receive a positive comment. However, how should you deal with a negative comment? You have to understand that negative comments are not completely bad. Although a negative comment might make you feel insulted, you should learn to relax when you read a negative comment. Try to find out if the said negative comment has any basis or not. You should realize that every negative comment is an opportunity to make improvements. However, there are also negative comments that are completely unreasonable. As a rule, this is how you should deal with a negative comment: If it is reasonable, then thank the one who commented as he/she helped you to improve. That is something that you should appreciate. However, if the negative comment was made simply to say something bad, you can either just ignore it or give a polite reply like a simple "Thank you." without having to explain anything else. After all, your other readers and followers will know if a certain comment is true or not.

If a person who commented on your work also has a blog, it is advised that you also visit his blog and comment on his posts. This is a good way to establish new connections and build a good relationship. After all, in the online world, bloggers usually help and support one another.

- Join related groups and forums

It is strongly advised that you join related online groups and forums. No matter what your business is, you will surely find related groups online. By joining these groups, you can connect with people who can be your potential clients or customers, as well as meet people who might be able to help you with your business. It is also free to join such groups online, and it usually takes just a few clicks of the mouse. Social media channels always have groups that you can join. With regard to forums, there are many forums online that. You can participate in it. Sometimes it also helps to just read the posts, and you will surely find some interesting posts from time to time.

- Be patient

Establishing your presence online or even just on social media will definitely take time. Even if you follow all the best blogging practices in the world, it will take some time before you can establish a strong following. Therefore, you have to be patient. Be patient and persevere. Do not worry; once you are able to establish your business online, it will be easier to get more work or projects.

- Connect with the right people

Connect with the right people. The quality of your connections can determine the extent of your reach in the market. The right people are those who have a strong following. Although quantity may also matter, it is more important to focus on the quality of your connections.

This does not mean that you should ignore other people. Rather, it just tells you where you should focus on.

Especially when you are just starting out, do not expect for these people to just connect with you. It is your job to take steps to find and connect with them. If you notice someone who has a good and strong following, then try to establish a connection with him. As we have already discussed, you can easily do this by writing a comment on his posts. Now, the key here is to write a grabbing comment that will make him/her take notice of you. If you get lucky, he might also comment and share your work with his network, and this is a great way to tap a wide network of new connections. Now, do this several times, and you will surely end up with a good following as long as you also do your part and provide quality information and/or service.

- Quality is your main priority

No matter what kind of business or online job you do, take note that quality remains to be the most important thing. In fact, even an article without any SEO techniques can gain lots of traffic provided it has a good quality, such as being able to provide helpful information and details. Now, whether you work as a freelancer or programmer or anything else, the way to have continuous business/projects is to render quality work. Otherwise, it will be hard for your client to refer you to another or to rehire your services.

A common mistake is to try to quickly set up your freelance career or online business. This has a tendency to end up with lots of low-quality stuff. You need to take your time, especially when you are just building your foundation. Do not rush the process.

- "You are the average of the five people around you."

This may not be directly related to the job that you have, but it has an effect on your performance. What this saying means is that you should be careful with the people with whom you associate with. Hence, it is advised that you associate with those who will make you feel more motivated and inspired. Surround yourself with positive and successful people, or at least with those who inspire you to be a better person. These are the people who have a strong influence in your life.

- Time management

Time is money. When you go to work, mostly, you will also be paid per hour. If you know the value of your time, then you would surely what to manage how you spend it. You should have a schedule that is conducive to your work. But, do not end up with a schedule that is full of nothing but work, remember that you also need to rest and take a break from time to time. You should manage your time properly, especially when you have a family. Take note that you also need to spend time with your spouse and kids, if any. After all, what good is all the work that you do if you just live only for yourself?

- Learn from your competitors

You should learn from your competitors. No matter what online business or freelance service that you offer, you will surely have some competitors. Business competition is part of the market. If there is no competition, then perhaps you are in the wrong market. Instead of feeling bad that other people offer a similar service or product as you do, you should learn from them. Do this by comparing your strengths and weaknesses. Again, the strengths and weaknesses of your business are relative to the strengths and weaknesses of your competitors. You should try to further improve your strengths. You should also work on your weaknesses; otherwise, you might get left behind the competition. Competition is not really a bad thing, depending on how you view it. If you use it to improve yourself and your business, then you can say that it is good and healthy.

- Take a break

It is good to be hardworking. In fact, you are encouraged to work hard and to always do your best. However, you need to understand that it will take time before you can achieve your objective and to be able to establish your freelance or online business. You also need to take a break. If you allow some time to clear your mind and give yourself a break, then you will be more effective. Now, a common mistake is to take a rest but then continue to think about your problems while on a break. This will only make you feel more stressed. When you take a break, use that time wisely to really take a break and relax. This is the best time for you to go on a vacation or even spend just a movie night at home with your family. The important thing is to relax and have fun. Do not worry; after the break, you are expected to work even harder.

Conclusion

Thanks for making it through to the end of this book. I hope it was informative and able to provide you with all of the tools you need to achieve your goals whatever they may be.

The next step is to apply everything that you have learned. It is time for you to take positive actions and make positive changes in your life.

This book is actually a journey of change. Indeed, by the time you take the last step, you have already made lots of wonderful changes. It should be noted that change is within your power to do, but it requires that you take actions to make them happen.

As you follow the lessons in this book, you will be faced with challenges and hardships, and this is also how you will see and appreciate your own strengths. Of course, it will also let you know about your weaknesses. Now, this is important. Some people shy away from knowing their weaknesses, and so they fail to do something about them. The more weaknesses that you are able to identify the more chances you have at improving yourself and your business. Indeed, this journey is not just about making more money, but it can also change your life for the best.

If you want to make changes in your life, then you need to take positive actions. You cannot just wait and expect for something to happen out of nowhere. You need to realize that you have the power to make things happen. You do not have to rely on anything else but yourself. You simply have to do your best, especially when you know that there are people who also depend on you for support. Still, even though you may have a family that relies on you, it does not mean that you should no longer strive to live the life that you have always wanted. After all, your family also wants you to be happy, and they want you to be successful. If you truly succeed in your chosen path whatever that may be, you will surely be in a far better position than you are right now. There is nothing that compares to a life where you are happy and satisfied with what you do and have. The thing is that you can have that life that you have always wanted. You simply have to give yourself a chance to achieve it. This book is your ticket that shows you the way to your dreams. However, knowledge alone is not enough. You have to put that knowledge into practice to take your dream into reality. Since this is a journey to achieve your dream life, it is only right that you give it your best.

Finally, if you found this book useful in anyway, a review on Amazon is always appreciated!

Passive Income

7 Predictable Ways to Generate a Passive Income Stream when you are over 40 and While Working a Full Time Job

Introduction

I want to thank you and congratulate you for downloading the book, *"Passive Income: 7 Predictable Ways to Generate a Passive Income Stream While Working a Full Time Job"*.

This book has actionable information on 7 predictable ways through which you can generate passive income while retaining your full-time job.

A passive income is any income earned from income streams that do not need consistent every day input. Traditionally, many used the term"passive income" in reference to income earned from investment vehicles such as stocks, dividends, rent, interest on monies, royalties, capital gains, etc. Thanks to technology, this definition has morphed. Today, while the definition of a passive income still remains the same, income generated from sources that do not require consistent output, in light of a society entrenched in working a day job for 8 or more hours 5 days a week, any income generated from working 2-3 hours a day can fit into the passive income description. Because of this and other reasons such as financial and time freedom, supplementation of income, unlimited income potential, and most importantly, being the 'boss,'creating a passive income stream to supplement, or even replace an active income has become the "it-thing" and thousands of people are now looking for ways to earn a passive income while working a day job.

Since you are reading this, undoubtedly, you would like to learn how to earn a passive income as a way to supplement your active income, or earn enough to leave the confines of your day job.

If this is what you desire, you're in luck because the internet has made the prospect easier and unlike days gone, to get started, you don't need thousands of dollars. All you need is a computer (or even a smartphone), and active internet connection, and 2-3 hours of your day for no less than 3 months. After this time (which is often how long it takes to setup an online-based, passive income-generating stream), you can work for as little as 4 hours a week and still earn well enough to quit your day job if you so wish.

In this book, we are going to discuss 7 highly potent, yet relatively easy to implement, online-based passive income streams you can implement while working a day job since they require minimal hours to setup (2-3 consistent hours per day).

The good thing about these passive income streams is that when you successfully implement one, you can move on to the others, and by so doing, create multiple passive income streams that take less than 4 hours per week to manage.

Thanks again for downloading this book. I hope you enjoy it!

Table of Contents

I won't go round in circles trying to justify why you should venture into passive income because given that you are reading this book, you perhaps have heard great things about passive income e.g. ease of scalability, the passive nature of the income, tax benefits etc., which has informed your decision to look out for ways to make passive income. Instead, we will immediately start by discussing the different strategies you can follow to make passive income in a step by step format.

1st Strategy: Blogging

Blogging is the most common and predictable way to earn a passive income. In fact, many of the other sources of online passive income anchor on blogs. In other words, if you have a blog that has a good enough readership, you can start and support almost all the other online passive income strategies that we will be discussing in this book.

Since you're not new to the internet, you have read success stories of bloggers such as Brett McKay of artofmanliness.com, John Chow of Johnchow.com, Mario Lavandeira of PerezHilton.com, and Pat Flynn of Smartpassiveincome.com, and other bloggers who earn thousands of dollars per month from blogging about topics and things they love. This goes to show you just how powerful blogging is as an income stream.

The good thing about blogging is that to get started, you need nothing but a passion, dedication (the willingness to dedicate 2-3 hours of your day to blogging), and a bit of easy to learn technical knowledge (which is where this book comes in). Here is how to go about it:

How to Start a Revenue-Generating Blog

In this guide, we are going to reveal how to use your free time (in the morning before heading to your day job or in the evening—morning works best because as Pat Flynn says, "always start your day by dedicating 2 hours to working for yourself) to create a blog that generates no less than $1,000 per month. Let's get to it:

Step 1: Choose a Topic/Niche

To set up a successful blog that earns you a passive income going into hundreds of thousands of dollars as you work your other job, sleep, or even travel, the first thing you need to do is choose a topic. Here, go with a topic that impassions you because at the end of the day, blogging should be fun and because it takes time to bear fruit—do not expect to make tons of money a month after starting—passion is a key ingredient because it ensures you stick to blogging when quitting seems like the best option.

With that said however, research from Wpromote shows that the top 5 most popular blog categories are music, fashion, travel, food, and beauty. While this also means these are the most competitive, you are free to go with what you feel most passionate about. At the end of the day, even if you chose a less competitive topic that does not impassion you, your chances of creating an income generating blog are very minimal since the prospect calls for patience and a lot of dedication. Once you have your topic of interest at hand...

Step 2: Choose a Domain and Hosting Option for Your Site

As indicated earlier, the greatest thing about blogging is that you do not need to invest anything other than your time; this is because if you choose to, you can use hosted blog option such as blogger.com, wordpress.com, or even squarespace.com. The downside to using these options is that while the hosting is free, the domain name is not brandable.
For instance, if you decide to create a blog about a specific genre of music such as reggae, and you choose to name your blog "one love reggae," if you go with the WordPress option, your domain name shall be "onelovereggae.wordpress.com. This, as you can see, is a mouthful. On the other hand, a self-hosted blog allows you to choose a brandable domain. Using the reggae example, the domain name would be onelovereggae.com. You can learn how to choose a domain name here.

A domain will cost you anywhere from $1-$15 per year while hosting will vary depending on the provider and the option you choose (BlueHost, iPage and HostGator have options starting from as little as $3 per month). This article has some great insight on how to settle on a hosting provider.

You shall also need to setup your blog and customize it as you see fit. Google these things—you will find tons of related information related to your chosen blogging platform. For instance, if you opt to use WordPress, the world's most popular blogging platform, you can get ideas on how to set up your WordPress blog from Siteground.com or WPbeginner.com.

Step 3: Start Writing and Driving Traffic to Your Blog

With your blog all set up, the next step is to start writing content. In the online space, content reigns supreme. This is because how unique, informational, and helpful to readers it is, and how well optimized it is for search bots will determine how popular your blog becomes and how much traffic it generates. More traffic equals more money potential.

When it comes to deciding what to blog about, your passion should come in handy and help you brainstorm topics. In terms of driving traffic to your blog, concentrate on being super helpful to readers by writing amazing content, and then optimize this content for search engines. This therefore means you have to conduct keyword research and use this to write for people and optimize your content for search. This is not as difficult as it sounds and with CMS (content management systems) such as WordPress, you will find tons of plugins (such as SEO Yoast) that shall help you with search engine optimization.

Another thing you should do here is create an editorial calendar so you avoid the mistake of blogging when you feel like it. Creating a revenue generating blog require consistency. Brainstorm 50-100 blog ideas and spread them out on calendar (aim for a blog a day since research has shown that frequently updated blogs attract more traffic).

Step 4: Monetize

When your blog starts attracting visitors, you are free to monetize it by creating products related to your blog. For instance, if your blog is on reggae, you can create a reggae guitar guide for beginners eBook), affiliate marketing, or make money with advertisements from ad networks like Chitika, Media.net, , Ad Maven, Vibrant Media, Clicksor, Advertising.com, Google Adsense, , Revenue Hits, Revcontent, AdBlade, Undertone, , PropellerAds, WWW Promoter, Infolinks, Adbuff etc. or targeted ads from companies fit your audience. As I already mentioned, many of the other blog monetization options like selling software, mobile apps, selling physical products, independent publishing, membership sites, information courses etc. can be anchored on a blog so make sure to take blogging seriously if you really want to end up making real money from blogging. The opportunities for making passive income when you have a blog are endless! Monetization options for a traffic generating blog are endless and once you get consistent traffic, you will have your fair share of picks.

More important than monetizing is making sure the blog is helpful to readers and friendly to search engines.

As you shall note, the other strategies we shall discuss here shall depend on how well you can implement this one strategy because without a blog/website, the other strategies shall be less effective.

To help you out further, here are various resources related to creating an income-generating blog:

How to choose a niche for your blog
http://www.bloggingwizard.com
http://www.wpsuperstars.net

How to set up a WordPress blog
(WordPress is the easiest to use CMS)
http://www.wpbeginner.com

How to drive traffic to a blog
http://neilpatel.com
https://www.iwillteachyoutoberich.com

DOWNLOAD YOUR FREE BONUS:
5 PASSIVE INCOME BUSINESS MODELS VIDEO COURSE

2nd Strategy: Affiliate Marketing

Affiliate marketing is an amazing way to generate a gushing stream of passive income. When well implemented, affiliate marketing can earn you hundreds of thousands of dollars per month, enough money to have you quit your day job and start doing whatever your heart desires.

Affiliate marketing is a business model where you "affiliate" yourself to products and services. In simple terms, this means you market other peoples' services and products and in exchange, whenever a customer you refer buys a product or service, you earn a percentage of the buying price. For instance, if you refer someone to a piece of software retailing for $500 and you have an affiliate relationship with the software company stipulating that for every referral, you will earn 20%, you will earn $100.

In the online space, the affiliate marketing business model uses special links called "affiliate links."Affiliate links are unique web links provided to affiliate marketers for marketing purposes. The link has a special cookie unique to you; the purpose of this cookie is to capture where the lead/referral is coming from so that when someone clicks on the link and buys something, the purchase reflects on your referral account and you can receive a commission for it.

Affiliate marketing offers exponential potential. For instance, if you have a popular reggae blog, you can affiliate yourself to reggae concerts sellers, guitar sellers, and other such companies that match your audience needs. You can do all this from the same website because to affiliate yourself, all you have to do is insert a link into a page or a post.

For instance, if you are writing a post title "10 amazing-sounding guitars ideal for reggae music," for each guitar on the list, you can drop an affiliate link to a retailer (make sure you have an affiliate relationship with the retailer), and when someone clicks on your affiliate link and makes a purchase, you shall earn a commission.

To get started on affiliate marketing, create a website or blog using the steps outlined in the previous strategy. Once the blog starts generating traffic on a consistent basis, decide which affiliate offers are a fit for your audience and affiliate yourself to these offers by inserting the affiliate links into your posts and pages.

You don't have to have a personal relationship with the companies that are recruiting affiliates. You can register in affiliate marketplaces i.e. websites that help publishers find advertisers. Some of the popular places you can register as an affiliate include the following:

ClickBank

CJ Affiliate by Conversant (Formerly known as Commission Junction)

ShareASale

Amazon Associates

EBay Partner Network

Rakuten Affiliate Network

Avangate

Revenue Wire

TradeDoubler

And many others

In accordance with the law, every time you insert an affiliate link into your content or page, insert a disclaimer letting readers know that by using the affiliate link to make a purchase, you will earn a commission.

Another way to go about affiliate marketing is using paid advertising. For instance, let us assume you would like to affiliate yourself to a "custom guitar" service. You can use paid advertising on platforms such as Google AdWords and social media platforms such as Instagram, Facebook, Twitter, and other paid advertising options to promote the service to the masses.

To be successful at affiliate marketing, and therefore, earn a passive income even as you sleep, you are better off operating from a blog or website because this allows for centralization and diversification. For instance, even when you want to use paid advertising to promote a custom guitar service, you are likely to be more successful if you create a post reviewing the service (from a personal perspective), and then promoting this post on social media. This will ensure that when the service becomes popular, that one post can earn you thousands of dollars year after year without needing any maintenance.

As a rule of thumb, do not affiliate yourself to product or services you do not use because when you do and the service and products you promote fail to work as implied, your reputation will suffer because the internet hates fraudsters. To achieve massive success with affiliate marketing, place your offers at strategic areas of your website and pages.

Let us look at an example:

Assume you have a website that has 50 posts generating 1,000 views per month (total traffic=50,000). Out of this, assume that each page has affiliate offers from different companies offering a $100 product. If your conversation rate is 1% per month (a 1% conversion rate is very easy to achieve), it means out of your 50,000 visitors, 500 will be clicking on your affiliate links and purchasing. If your affiliate relationship with these providers stipulates that you earn 10% of the purchase price, each conversion shall earn you $10 and therefore, you shall earn more than $5, 000 each month.

The affiliate marketing process is as follows:

1. Drive massive amounts of traffic to your website.

2. Find affiliate programs and offers that fit your audience.

3. Insert your affiliate links into your wildly popular posts and pages while making sure that this insertion adds value to readers' lives.

4. Be open about your affiliate relationship by adding an affiliate disclaimer to each affiliate offer.

5. Optimize your conversion rate so you can convert as many of your web visitors as possible.

If you can do the above and find well-paying offers, you will be well on your way to earning money as you commute, travel, work at your day job, or even sleep. What a life!

Further reading

https://www.locationrebel.com

http://nichehacks.com

MonetizePros.com.

http://www.affiliatebible.com

http://www.wpeagle.com

Myworkfromhomemoney.com

NeilPatel.com

3rd Strategy: Membership Sites

A membership site is a blog-like website where members pay a monthly fee to access premium content not freely available on the blog section of the website.

Contrary to popular belief, creating a membership site does not require tons of technical knowledge such as web design or coding because with WordPress, you can use plugins to bar some information and make it available to paying members. One of the greatest things about a membership site is the recurrent nature of the business.

As an example, if the barred content you create for membership site is eBooks, podcasts, video and audio webinars, or virtual conferences, if you keep the information fresh and updated (for example, you offer webinars and conferences on a daily, weekly, or even monthly basis), if you keep the information valuable, paid members will keep paying the membership fee.

To get started, create a website/blog as indicated earlier. For this purpose, you can create WordPress based website (it's easier to manage thanks to plugins and an easy to use interface) and install a membership plugin such as MemberPress or S2member (simply search the plugin on the plugins search bar). The plugin shall guide you through the process of adding the product and payment options. Make sure this information is very relevant your web visitors and compels them to want to pay to join your membership site. Make sure that creating a username and password is easy and seamless too because if the process is not easy, users will be at odds and your conversion rate may suffer. You can also create various levels of membership options.

Creating a successful membership site depends on the following.

The first thing you have to do is build trust: no one wants to buy something from someone he or she does not know or trust. The best way to do this is to offer freebies such as trial or free content. For instance, assuming your website is on self-development, you can create free self-development content for your site as a way to build trust and show readers that if you have such valuable information on your free blog, the information restricted to members is infinitely better. This will make it easier for web visitors to subscribe to your membership and pay the monthly fee.

As obvious as it sounds, the key to success in this venture is to drive traffic to your site (traffic is central to all online-based, passive income strategies discussed here). To ensure you convert these visitors into paid members, create an effective lead magnet. A lead magnetis a bribe in the form of upgrades, freebies, and signup incentives that gets people to give you their contact information such as email and name. For instance, besides the free content, you can offer a free consultation.

Let us look at an example:

Assume you have a members only self-improvement blog where you have three levels: the free level, level one that offers premium content every month, level 2 that offers free content and 2 coaching sessions per month, and level 3 that offers weekly coaching sessions.

Assume that your site attracts 200,000 visitors per month. Out of these, 100,000 go for the free content. Out of the remaining 100,000, you convert 1% (1,000 people) as follows: 950 choose level 1 priced at $49 per month (total=$46,550), 30 choose level 2 priced at $99 per month (total=$2,970), and 20 choose level 3 priced at $299 per month (total=5,980), your total earning shall be $55, 500, which is not bad at all. Since the bulk of this revenue shall be from level 1 that does not require one on one consulting, you can use your weekend to create content for them.

As for the rest, you can schedule them into your calendar accordingly. If you give each of person a 30-minute consulting session and work for 2 hours every day (serving 4 people per day except on weekend), a month shall be enough time to offer premium one-on-one services that leave your client happy.

Once you reach such a point, you can take off the pressure by delegating tasks. For instance, you can outsource the creation of the premium content (after drafting it of course), uploading it to the site, customer service for member response, social media marketing and management, and simply concentrate on offering one on one coaching. This shall help you grow your business to a point where if you so want, you can quit your day job and concentrate on the membership site full time (thereby increasing your earning potential). The beauty of membership sites is that they work across all niches and as long as people are interested in a specific topic and you can create highly valuable content on the same, you can earn money from it. For instance, you can create a membership site offering premium freelance writing jobs.

Further reading

http://theworldismyoffice.com
http://www.wpbeginner.com
https://www.inc.com
https://ontraport.com

4th Strategy: Kindle Publishing

Of the passive income strategies we shall discuss here, this is the only one that does not necessarily demand a website. And the good news about it is that you can make your first sale as a complete beginner within less than 24 hours!

Publishing books has always been profitable; so profitable in fact, that traditional publishers are constantly giving new writers book advances running into seven figures. The good news is that to create a publishing empire, you do not necessarily need to go the traditional publishing way especially considering that getting a publisher is not a stroll in the park. You can self-publish on Kindle.

Kindle publishing (Kindle Direct Publishing) is the publishing arm of technology giant Amazon. Launched in 2007, KDP as its abbreviated helps authors independently publish their book to Amazon's 193 million monthly visitors.

Kindle publishing, like affiliate marketing, offers unlimited potential especially if you are looking to publish more than one book (which you should if you want to earn thousands of dollars from the prospect). Here is everything you need to know about creating a passive income-generating kindle publishing empire:

Step 1: Choose a Niche

Your success as a Kindle publisher shall depend on your ability to find profitable niches topics on which to write books. The great thing here is that to do so, you need not look further than Amazon. No matter how great a writer you are, if you write a book on a topic that lacks readership, topic readers' want solutions to, you will be shooting yourself in the foot.

Here, the easiest thing you can do is think of a problem you would like to solve. Here is a secret no other passive income book shall tell you: ***if you are truly committed to creating lasting streams of passive income, you have to solve a problem people are willing to pay to solve***.

Once you have a problem in mind, visit the <u>Kindle Best seller site</u>. On the left hand side, you are going to see categories. Choose a category you think you can write a book on (or one that matches the problem you want to solve). If you are yet to decide which problem to tackle, simply choose a category you consider appealing.

When you navigate to a specific category, you will head deeper into that category and you may find other sub-categories. For instance, if you decide to go with self-help, under it, you will see other sub-categories such as creativity, eating disorders, happiness, etc. Choose one you want to scrutinize further and keep digging until you get to the sub niches.

As an example, below are the top 100 books in the niche self-help and sub-niche eating disorder and body image. Once you're in the bestseller niche and sub-niche, look for patterns. Can you notice 2 or more books on related topics? If you notice 2 or more books on a related topic, this is an indicator that this topic is popular and doing well.

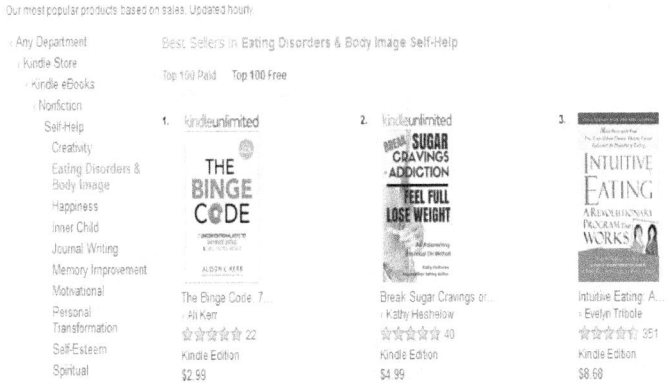

The next step is to dig further. Amazon Kindle ranks books according to their download and reviews. A popular and often downloaded book will have a higher rank with 1 being the most downloaded book.

When you notice related books, click on each book (you can open different tabs on your browser), and then scroll down; you will see the book rank. For instance, from the above, we see that binge eating is a popular topic because at the time of writing this, the 1st book (Binge eating code), the 4th book (brain over binge), and several other books (3rd, 9th, 13th, 14th, and several others) are on the list of 100.

The next step is to open some of these books to see their rank. At the time of writing this, Binge eating code ranks at 14, 477 in the entire Kindle store. Intuitive eating ranks at 17, 374, and Brain over Binge ranks at 18,168 respectively. This rank changes every minute (Amazon updates it every 6 hours).

Product details

File Size: 3740 KB
Print Length: 188 pages
Page Numbers Source ISBN: 1999786408
Simultaneous Device Usage: Unlimited
Publisher: MindFree; 1 edition (July 6, 2017)
Publication Date: July 6, 2017
Sold by: Amazon Digital Services LLC
Language: English
ASIN: B073HDB6ZN
Text-to-Speech: Enabled
X-Ray: Not Enabled
Word Wise: Enabled
Lending: Not Enabled
Enhanced Typesetting: Not Enabled
Amazon Best Sellers Rank: #14,477 Paid in Kindle Store (See Top 100 Paid in Kindle Store)
   #1 in Kindle Store > Kindle eBooks > Nonfiction > Self-Help > Eating Disorders & Body Image
   #9 in Books > Health, Fitness & Dieting > Mental Health > Eating Disorders
   #36 in Kindle Store > Kindle eBooks > Health, Fitness & Dieting > Diets & Weight Loss > Diets > Weight Maintenance

Product details

File Size: 3297 KB
Print Length: 369 pages
Page Numbers Source ISBN: 1250004047
Publisher: St. Martin's Griffin; 3 edition (August 7, 2012)
Publication Date: August 7, 2012
Sold by: Amazon Digital Services LLC
Language: English
ASIN: B006ZL3P4G
Text-to-Speech: Enabled
X-Ray: Enabled
Word Wise: Enabled
Lending: Not Enabled
Screen Reader: Supported
Enhanced Typesetting: Enabled
Amazon Best Sellers Rank: #17,374 Paid in Kindle Store (See Top 100 Paid in Kindle Store)

    #3 in Kindle Store > Kindle eBooks > Nonfiction > Self-Help > Eating Disorders & Body Image
    #5 in Kindle Store > Kindle eBooks > Medical eBooks > Special Topics > Nutrition
    #13 in Books > Health, Fitness & Dieting > Mental Health > Eating Disorders

Product details

File Size: 1215 KB
Print Length: 328 pages
Publisher: Camedia Publishing (January 1, 2011)
Publication Date: January 1, 2011
Sold by: Amazon Digital Services LLC
Language: English
ASIN: B005F9UZ1U
Text-to-Speech: Enabled
X-Ray: Enabled
Word Wise: Enabled
Lending: Not Enabled
Screen Reader: Supported
Enhanced Typesetting: Enabled
Amazon Best Sellers Rank: #18,168 Paid in Kindle Store (See Top 100 Paid in Kindle Store)

    #4 in Kindle Store > Kindle eBooks > Nonfiction > Self-Help > Eating Disorders & Body Image
    #15 in Books > Health, Fitness & Dieting > Mental Health > Eating Disorders
    #214 in Kindle Store > Kindle eBooks > Biographies & Memoirs > Memoirs

The idea here is to look for related books that are ranking well. If several related books rank at 1>20,000, this is a niche worth pursuing; it means the book ranking at 20,000 is selling a minimum of 3-15 books per day. The screenshot below shows the Kindle rank in relation to book sales and potential incomes.

Kindle Book Rank

- ✓ Rank 50,000 to 100,000— selling 0— 1 book a day.
- ✓ Rank 10,000 to 50,000— selling 3 to 15 books a day.
- ✓ **Rank 5,500 to 10,000— selling 15 to 30 books a day.**
- ✓ Rank 3,000 to 5,500— selling 30 to 50 books a day.
- ✓ ***Rank 500 to 3,000— selling 50 to 200 books a day***
- ✓ Rank 350 to 500— selling 200 to 300 books a day.
- ✓ Rank 100 to 350— selling 300 to 500 books a day.
- ✓ Rank 35 to 100— selling 500 to 1,000 books a day.
- ✓ Rank 10 to 35— selling 1,000 to 2,000 books a day.
- ✓ Rank of 5 to 10— selling 2,000 to 4,000 books a day.
- ✓ Rank of 1 to 5— selling 4,000 + books a day.

Once you find a niche, you have to come up with a title and subtitle for your book and then brainstorm and mindmap your ideas for the book. Fully flesh the mind map until you have a table of content like structure for your book.

Step 2: Write the Book, Create Cover, and Publish

With your mind map at hand, you will notice that your book will most likely write itself and from there, you can dedicate yourself to writing 1,000 words of your book per day. In about 10 days, you will have a publish-worthy book. Once done with the first draft, edit the book a first, second, and third time; if possible, hire an editor. Talking about hiring someone to write your book:

The most amazing thing about the Kindle publishing strategy is that even if you are not the creative type, you can hire someone to write the book for you. You will find great freelancers on site such as Upwork.com, Freelancer.com, WriteArticlesForMe.com, EpicWrite.com, TheWritingSummit.com and other platforms. Once the book is ready, hire someone to create a book cover on Fiverr.com (or do it yourself if you have the expertise), sign up for <u>Kindle Publishing, and follow the prompts to publish your book</u>.

Step 3: Market the Book

Like most passive income businesses, how much you end up earning from Kindle publishing will depend on how much traffic you can drive to your book. The more exposure your book gets, the better it is likely to perform and the more revenue you are bound to generate.

To market your book, you can use options such as social media, free and paid book promos, paid advertising, guest blogging, and other such ideas.

Let us look at an example:

Assume you create 5 great books that rank at 10,000. This means you shall be selling 15 books of each title each day. Depending on your price point (how you price the book—go for nothing below $2.99 so you can take 70% of the <u>revenue share</u>), you shall be earning

$156.957 from the five books per day (70/100 X $ 2.99= $2.093 X 15 books sold each day X 5 book titles= $156.957 per day). This therefore means on a good month, you can take home $4000+. This is not bad considering the effort and the fact that after publishing the book, marketing it will require less than 30 minutes per day.

Further reading

https://kindlepreneur.com
http://okdork.com
https://www.tckpublishing.com
https://www.thecreativepenn.com

DOWNLOAD YOUR FREE BONUS:
5 PASSIVE INCOME BUSINESS MODELS VIDEO COURSE

Go To: http://bit.ly/5PassiveIncome

5th Strategy: YouTube Videos

Never before has man loved video than he does now. Today, videos are the most consumed form of online content. From funny cat videos, to game walkthroughs, to makeup videos, video is the "it-thing." And in the world of video, nothing beats YouTube.

Owned by Google, and boasting of over 30 million visitors per day, YouTube is a prime way to generate a passive income. How do you go about this? What do you need to do to become a YouTube millionaire? Let us discuss this:

Step 1: Setup Your Account and Start Creating Content

This one is very straightforward: create an account on YouTube. The process is very straightforward, as <u>all you need is a Google Account</u>. As you do so, however, you may want to pay attention to the nature of your YouTube channel (the topics you shall be covering) and if possible, have the name reflect on the title of your channel. For instance, if you intend to create videos that motivate people, you could name your channel something along the lines of "dailymotivation."

When thinking about which types of videos to create, remember to follow your passion or ask yourself a question such as "what do I know and can teach easily?" This will help you come up with an idea for a channel. The idea here is simple: come up with a channel people will find helpful; this does not necessarily mean that the channel and the videos you create have to be educational. Always remember that if people are actively searching for specific information, you can create video content for it irrespective of whether what they are searching for is funny videos or even weird videos.

When you start creating content, make sure the content is valuable enough to attract views and shares. As an example, the world seems to like videos of "unboxing/reviewing products." If you can buy niche products (products such as vapes), unbox them, and then show people how to use them, you have something on your hands, provided the videos you create are clear and helpful. The good thing about creating YouTube videos is that if you cannot afford expensive shooting cameras, you can get started with the camera on your high-end smartphone.

Step 2: Drive Traffic to the Channel/Video

After creating 10 or 20 videos and uploading them to your channel (do this immediately after creating your channel and before you start promoting it), hit the road and start marketing your channel and the specific videos you have created. The best way to do this is to share the videos on social media (you can even use paid advertising to promote the video to its relevant target audience), or share the video on your blog (see how they two relate?).

The following resources shall teach you optimize your channel for search as well as how to promote your YouTube channel:
https://blog.hootsuite.com
https://www.outbrain.com

Step 3: Monetize

After building your fan and subscriber base and reached 10,000 per video, add monetization to your channel to start making money.

Monetizing YouTube is relatively easy because all you have to do is allow Google to serve ads on your channel/videos (the material has to be non-copyrighted).

The monetization option is on your YouTube sidebar on the channel, status, and features option (you have to be logged is as a YouTube publisher). From here, simply enable monetization.

Once you have this setup, you are ready to start earning from YouTube. Let us look at an example:

YouTube pays through Google AdSense through a CPM (cost per Mille or cost per thousand). This means they pay for every 1,000-ad impressions. The CPM for each impression may be $0.1 to $10 depending on the niche you are serving.

Here is how the math would look if we go with a $0.1 CPM:

1,000 views=$0.1
10,000 views=$1
100,000 views=$10
1,000,000 views=$100
10,000,000 views=$1,000
100,000,000 views=$10,000
1,000,000,000 views=$100,000

As you can see, how much you end up earning from YouTube will depend on your ad impression, which shall depend on how many views you can drive to your website; therefore, the more traffic you drive to your channel and videos, the higher the earning potential.

One of the greatest thing about YouTube is that once the video is live and generating views, the multiplication factor is great and in most instances, the video shall market itself (especially if it's good) through person-to-person sharing and social shares:

Further reading

https://www.quora.com
https://www.entrepreneur.com
https://creatoracademy.youtube.com
https://monetizepros.com
https://www.incomediary.com

DOWNLOAD YOUR FREE BONUS:
**5 PASSIVE INCOME BUSINESS
MODELS VIDEO COURSE**

Go to:http://bit.ly/5PassiveIncome

6th Strategy: Ecommerce Site

One thing we know for sure is that how we shop has changed. Today, many of us would rather shop online. This has precipitated the rise of ecommerce moguls who are earning millions of dollars per month. Here, think along the lines of Amazon, Alibaba, eBay, Etsy, Baidu, and other similar ones.

You too can start such a business without having to give up your day job. Here is how:

Step 1: Decide What to Sell

The prospect of creating a successful ecommerce site hinges on having something to sell; without a product, getting started will not be easy. This pays credence to the importance of having a great product to sell.

The best way to go about deciding what to sell is to create something that solves a problem (solving a problem is central to online success) or take something in existence, make it better and then market it better. The second option is easier if you are not a creator.

When choosing a product, pay attention to niches you find familiar and are passionate about because selling something you are not familiar with means you will waste a lot of time trying to figure out how to connect with, or sell to the target audience. When you restrict yourself to a niche you are familiar with, you make this process much easier.Amazon is a great place to look for niche ideas for ecommerce sites.

The following resources should help you with finding the perfect products for your ecommerce store:

https://www.shopify.com
https://www.shopify.com
https://www.bigcommerce.com
https://www.ecomdash.com

Step 2: Source the Product

Those already making money in the ecommerce scene will willingly tell you that Alibaba is the best place to source for products. To use Alibaba, all you have to do is head to the site, type in the main keywords for the product you chose, and choose manufacturers who meet your specific criteria. As a rule, go with gold suppliers.

Step 3: Set up Your Store and Start Selling

Once you have a supplier for your product, the next step is to create your store. Here, you can create a store on sites such as Amazon, Etsy, eBay or Shopify, or create your own ecommerce website. Here, if you know nothing about ecommerce, you can recruit a capable web designer on sites such as Upwork.com or Freelancer.com and others.

After setting up your site, start uploading content descriptions for your merchandise and selling. To sell, however,

To drive traffic to you ecommerce site, you can use paid advertising (as long as the return on investment is ok), or seek organic traffic by performing SEO on the site content.

As an example, if you create a store than offers 5 products priced at $20, of which you 100 products per month per product, if the initial cost of creating and shipping the product is $10, it means in a month, your gross profit could be $5,000, give or take. This is without having to work tons of hours to generate the same.

Further Reading

https://ecommerce-platforms.com
http://www.huffingtonpost.com
https://www.shopify.com
https://www.oberlo.com
https://www.shopify.com

7th Strategy: Service Arbitrage Business

The other way you can generate a passive income is by selling other people's service, i.e. you act as a paid intermediary between those seeking services and those selling them. The best example of such sites is most freelancing websites such as Upwork.com, Fiverr.com, iWriter.com, Freelancer.com and the likes.

The idea behind this is relatively simple: find people looking to offer specific services online, services such as writing, find clients willing to pay for the same services at a rate higher than the one asked by the service provider, connect the two (preferably through a web portal) and pocket the difference.

Getting started on this business model is easy and very straightforward: all you need is to choose the service you want to arbitrage. This could be a service such as SEO analysis, book covers, social media management and marketing, etc. Once you have this core service in mind, start looking for service providers offering such services. You can find many of these on freelancing sites and then foster a relationship with them.

The next step is to search for clients looking for people seeking these services, offer to provide the services at a rate higher than what you shall offer the service provider and voila, you are in business. The greatest thing about this is that it does not require much time or much from you in terms of monetary investment.

For instance, if you decide to arbitrage "SEO analysis services," you can find a great service provider who is willing to offer amazing SEO services at $1,000 and on the other hand, a company that is willing to pay someone $1,500 for the same service. If you sell yourself as a great service provider for this company, and if the person you hire does an amazing job, you can earn $500 from being an intermediary.

The down side to this type of business is that it will take a substantial amount of time to create a convincing profile for the specific service you are offering. However, if you are good at this, which you can manage—creating trust and credibility—by creating an amazing portfolio site for the specific service you are arbitraging, you can be well on your way to earning thousands of dollars per week.

For instance, assume that it takes you about 6 months to create a great portfolio site for SEO analysis service and that on a weekly basis, 3 web owners reach out for your services (because you have already established yourself as an authority on the subject) paying $1500 each. If you outsource the same service to your capable service provider for $1,000, you can pocket the difference, which is $1,500 for the three clients. If this holds week-in-week-out, you can earn $4,500 with the potential to earn so much more as your business grows.

The most amazing thing about service arbitrage is that it is labor free: all you have to do is find service providers, find companies seeking the services offered by these service providers, offer the services and once the contract is yours, simply offer it to the service provider at a lesser fee. While it sounds fraudulent, there is nothing fraudulent about it just as there is nothing wrong about retail arbitrage.

Further reading

https://www.entrepreneurs-journey.com
https://www.warriorforum.com

Conclusion

We have come to the end of the book. Thank you for reading and congratulations for reading until the end.

This book has shown you 7 ways to create a passive income online. Implement these ways one after the other (setting up most requires less than 3 hours of work per day, which you can do before or after work), and in 6 months to 1 year, your business should be at a point where it earns you a steady income without the need for every day work.

When you get to that point, you shall be financially free and stable.

If you found the book valuable, can you recommend it to others? One way to do that is to post a review on Amazon.

Click here to leave a review for this book on Amazon!

Thank you and good luck!

DOWNLOAD YOUR FREE BONUS:
5 PASSIVE INCOME BUSINESS MODELS VIDEO COURSE

Go to:http://bit.ly/5PassiveIncome

I need your help......

Thank you for purchasing and reading this book, I sincerely hope that you find value in the techniques and implement them into your life.

I created this book to help people start the journey of creating and building passive income streams. My goal is to let people know what options are available to them so that they can take advantage of them.

If you did find value in the book please take a minute to review the book and give your feedback as to what was good about and where it could improve.

This will help me in 2 ways:

1. It will help people decide if this book is worth buying.

2. Your feedback will help me make changes and improve the book.

High Income Producing Skills

7 Skills And Habits That Will Generate A 6 Figure Income

Introduction

I want to thank you and congratulate you for downloading the book, "*High Income Producing Skills: 7 Skills And Habits That Will Generate A 6 Figure Income*".
This book has actionable information on the 7 skills and habits that you can develop to help you generate a 6 figure income.

They say money cannot buy happiness (which is true) but the truth is, there is something that financial abundance can give you that very few things in the world can. In other words, financial abundance can create a conducive environment for happiness to thrive because happiness cannot just thrive on its own; it needs the right environment for it to develop and thrive.

This explains why we all strive to attain financial independence with the hopes that it will make us happy. Living a comfortable life, free from the worries brought about by financial instability and insecurity is definitely a goal worth keeping. With financial stability comes the freedom to live life the way you want, not having to worry about micromanaging your little available income.

Unfortunately, as you are well aware, financial independence does not come easy. In fact, many are the times when we try multiple times only to fail repeatedly. What's funny however is just how some people are able to attain financial freedom within a short period yet others live until their retirement years without ever attaining financial independence. What makes the difference?

Well, the secret is in building the right habits because as Will Durant put it, "*We are what we repeatedly do. Excellence, then, is not an act, but a habit.*" For you to attain financial independence, you have to build the right financial habits to propel you to the success you want. It starts with building habits that enable you to make more money first! And if you combine the right habits with some skills, you can be sure that you will rocket-fuel yourself to anything you want to become. This book will give you actionable information on 7 skills and habits that you can build to build a 6 figure income. Let's begin.

Thanks again for downloading this book. I hope you enjoy it!

Table of Contents

Before we discuss the skills and habits that you can build to put you on the path to a 6 figure income, let's start by building an understanding of how having the right skills and habits helps you to earn a 6 figure income.

Chapter 1: How Having the Right Skills and Habits Helps You Earn a 6 Figure Income

If there are 2 people, one who has been a lumberjack all his life and another who was just handed a saw and has never cut a tree his entire life, which of the two do you think will cut a big tree faster? Well, naturally, the first guy would definitely get it done fast mainly because he has the necessary expertise to cut trees.

This principle applies in all other aspects of life i.e. you can only get the most stuff done well if you have the necessary skills to actually do what needs to be done to propel you to the success you are looking for. The above example clearly shows that having the right skill is essential if you want to do a job the right way and fulfill your goal. As such, whatever your objective is, you need to find the right skill you need to build, to achieve it and then work on developing it. If your goal is to earn a 6 figure income, there are certain special skills that can help you fulfill it faster.

Before we get to a point of discussing these skills, let's first discuss why it is critical to have the right skills to excel in life.

As you are well aware, a skill simply refers to the ability to carry out a task really well. You can think of it as expertise in a certain area. When you have a certain skill, you can do a certain task in a better, more effective and efficient manner compared to if you don't have the necessary skill. Why is that so? Well, the truth is; that certain skill helps bring the following changes in you and your productivity.

- When you have a certain skill, you are able to understand certain tasks better. This in turn makes it easier for you to execute such tasks with greater ease, effectiveness and efficiency. As a result, you can be sure of better quality output within a shorter period. Let me use an example of baking a pie; if you have never baked a pie before, you are quite likely to make a terrible pie in the first attempt even if you know the steps that you need to take (e.g. are following a written recipe). Yes, you can improve with practice but who knows the number of attempts it will take you perfect your pie. However, if you take a baking course (online or offline) and do it consistently, you will soon have good baking skills, which will enable you to bake a nice pie easily. Through training, you will become aware of the different baking hacks and tricks that will help you avoid making mistakes while baking. All this will ultimately work together to ensure you have a great pie.

That's not all; when you have the right skill for performing a certain task, you are able to do it in a record time without compromising on quality. Think of driving for instance; if you are still a beginner driver, you will be very mechanical in what you are doing to an extent that you will end up driving unnecessarily slow. That's unlike being an experienced driver; with years of experience in driving, driving comes naturally to you and you don't waste time in making decisions while driving. If I drive the point home to something related to making money; if you are a beginner programmer for instance, you are likely to take hours upon hours in creating a functioning website, software, app, plug in etc. But if you are good at what you do because you have the necessary skills, you won't take too much time getting things done. This essentially means you can complete your clients' requests within a short period so that you can take more work. The same applies to having skills like copyrighting; as a pro, you will undoubtedly take less time to complete a single project compared to someone who is just getting started.

- With increased efficiency and speed comes greater productivity. This also sets ground for the establishment of new skills and scouting of new opportunities. Think about it for a moment; if you are a software developer, you could start by using your skill to land customers who will pay you to develop websites/software for them. With time, you may realize that you will no longer be trading your hours for money and instead opt to create software for doing different tasks, which you monetize through subscriptions for instance. What I mean here is that with the right skill, you can spin it off to your advantage to change with the changing times. For instance, Elon Musk developed his skills for coding at an early age. He even created his first video game at

12 years! He didn't know what he wanted to do at that time, but he knew that he needed to have the right skill to figure out what he aspired to have and then achieved it. As a coder, he spearheaded the formation of PayPal, which revolutionized online payment. Had Musk not worked on building the 'coding' skill, it is quite likely he would have never have been part of the team that founded PayPal and went on to become a billionaire.

From the above explanation, you can see that a skill provides you with the necessary expertise, knowledge and power you need to set yourself up for success in whichever way possible.

For these skills to come to fruition, you need to nurture the right habits to support the whole process of skill development and nurturing if you want to achieve your goals without fail.

The Place Of Habits In Building Your Earnings Potential

As important it is to have the right skill to create the necessary avenues to make money, it is equally important to nurture success yielding habits that can propel you towards the success you aspire to have. Man is a creature of habit so whatever we do, whoever we are and the life we have manifested for ourselves is because of our habits. If you feel miserable about your current life, find difficult in managing the household expenses and are nowhere near the financial independence you desire to have, it is because you don't have the right habits that draw financial success and abundance your way. You are likely to be lazy, procrastinate a lot, think negatively, set no goals for yourself and don't practice things to improve. Obviously, even if you have the necessary skills, if you always procrastinate, think negatively of yourself and have a host of other undesirable habits, you can be sure that you won't go far in life.

That's why if you wish to be successful in life and earn a 6 figure income, and even more than that, you need to work on building these success yielding habits. This book will discuss these habits along with 7 skills that will undoubtedly put you centrally at the path to a 6 figure income.

Let's begin with the first skill: copywriting.

Chapter 2: Skill #1- Copywriting

With the world increasingly becoming a global village, more than ever, the skill of copywriting has become one of the most sought after skills the world over! Individuals and corporates the world over are looking for great writers who can weave content in a way that resonates with the target audience and triggers the needed response. Forget marketers and advertisers; there are guys behind the scenes that develop/write the copy before it is taken up by marketers. Those are the guys that organizations and individuals looking to have an edge over the competition are looking for. And you could be that person!

This high demand explains why copywriting is one of the highest paid professions. While you may assume a copywriter does not make a decent income, this is only true for one with average writing skills. There are brilliant copywriters who make thousands of dollars each month just based on their copywriting skills.

So what exactly is copywriting and how can it help you earn a 6 figure income? Let's discuss that:

What is Copywriting?

In its simplest terms, copywriting is simply writing advertising and promotional material. I already stated that there is a guy behind every great advert, product description, product review, email, blog post, or other promotional material. If you are a copywriter, you are that guy who creates content for billboards, brochures, emails, websites, catalogs, flyers, any promotional material such as pens, caps and mugs and anything else that can be used to advertise a certain good or service. The text that is written by a copywriter is known as a copy and copywriting is a part of a staggering $2.3 trillion direct-response industry all across the globe.

Unlike editorial writing, copywriting is about encouraging the reader to take the desired action, which is usually to make a purchase of the good or service being promoted/advertised. It can also be to opt-in or become involved in some way with the good being advertised or the company being talked about. For instance, if a certain flyer encourages you to do volunteer work in a shelter home, that is its call to action.

Since a copywriter's job is to persuade the reader to take the desired action and convince him/her to use the said product or service (or take a certain action), he/ she is often known as 'salesman in print.' Just like the typical salesman tries to woo a potential customer so he/she actually makes the purchase, a copywriter does the same with the only difference being that a salesman uses his/her antics directly and face-to-face whereas a copywriter uses his/her written words in the copy to do the same.

Just to clarify: Copywriting is not the same as 'copyright"; the two are entirely different. Copyright refers to having the exclusive legal right to create, reproduce, sell, distribute or publish a certain piece of work such as music, artistic item or a book. A copyright protects that material and ensures it isn't used illegally without the authorization of its rightful owner. Any material with this symbol © is designated as a copyrighted material.

I know you might be wondering; but how the heck will you make six figures writing copy when the competition is so fierce even from oversees copywriters who can write just well but at a fraction of the rates you are going to charge?

Let's discuss that:

Yes, copywriting is indeed a skill that can help you make a six-figure income and even millions of dollars and there are scores of copywriters who are currently earning six figures writing sales copies for their clients. However, how much you make with this skill depends entirely on the amount of effort and time you invest into it.

Joshua Boswell is one of the popular copywriters who make six figure incomes from copywriting. His story is unique especially because he grew his copywriting business to more than $100,000 a year in as little as 1 year! Danny Margulies is another copywriter who's known for earning over six figures a year, as a freelance copywriter. Ed Gandia has also done it, after 27 months of working his butt off to build his copywriting skill! Clayton Makepeace is another big name in the industry who writes copies that **have made over $1.5 billion!**

There are countless other examples of people who have made and are still making six figures by leveraging on their copywriting skills. You too can be one of those who start and build your skill to become a six figure copywriter.

On average, a median copywriter with an average skill makes about $47,838 per year and 80% of all copywriters earn between $35k and $65k annually. However, this number increases as your expertise and experience improves.

I know you might be wondering; so why would anyone pay anybody so much money anyway?

Well, the number one reason why copywriting is a huge industry is because there is always something to sell. There are scores of people and corporations that want to get their word out there and get people to respond favorably to their message in order to ultimately increase leads and ultimately sales and profits. Since a lot of money goes into running an advertising/promotional campaign, it would be foolhardy not to invest in a good copy to ensure the message actually brings about the intended response from the audience. As you well know, promotional/advertising campaigns are expected to bring in millions or even billions of dollars for the respective companies. Unfortunately, these companies (advertisers) cannot achieve that if their copy is wanting. That's where copywriting skills come in. And as different companies plan to rake in millions or even billions of dollars in sales or profits, that's where copywriters make their kill!

For you to get to a point of making six figures, you should consistently be able to write a copy that gets the target audience to take whatever action you want them to take without them feeling coerced. The more persuasive your content is, the more customers it will lure in, the more the product will sell and the more you will succeed in this business. It is as simple as that.

Let me give an example; the restaurant industry in the U.S. alone spends over $5.875 billion on advertising every year. Since copywriting is a huge component of advertising, you can well imagine how much a good copywriter can make. This is just the statistic related to the restaurant industry. The automobile, agriculture, medical, pharmaceutical, education and many other industries spend a huge amount on advertising and copywriting every year too.

Therefore, if you wish to make 6 figures from copywriting, it is time you start paying more attention to building this skill so you can build and enhance your copywriting skills because as

you well know, there is lots of money to make!
The question is:

What Do You Need to Do to Become a Copywriter?

There are three amazing things about being a
copywriter:

- You can make a 6-figure income through it

- You can work from the comfort of your own
  home

- You don't have to have a college degree or
  some special qualifications to become a
  copywriter.

These three make copywriting one of those
professions where anybody can start and be
great at it! It is unlike many other professions
out there, which require years of formal
training to actually 'qualify' to offer your
services! With copywriting however, you just
have to have a unique flare with words to excel
at it! Let's take the discussion a little further:

1: Understand the Landscape

There has been an enormous surge in online
content over the past decade, which has created
an unprecedented demand for excellent
copywriters. A well-written sales copy on a

company's website not only provides prospective customers with confidence to buy that advertised good or service, it also enables businesses to easily generate organic web traffic from search engines.

Internet marketing is quite diverse and is moving at a dynamic pace. Copywriters who comprehend the latest trends in copywriting, social media and search engine optimization (SEO have an edge over copywriters who aren't aware of these trends. Therefore, if you wish to become a successful copywriter, you must make yourself comfortable with these trends first. Carry an extensive research on the copywriting trends and strategies in this day and age, and go through them time and again. The more you read about it, the better you will grasp the strategies and trends. You could even enroll for an online course (on Udemy for instance) on some of these things to build a strong understanding of the trends. If you wish not to sign up for a course, you can buy a book on Amazon, watch YouTube tutorials on the same and follow blogs on these trends to ensure you are not left behind. The truth is; it may take some time to settle in, but if you are consistent, you will soon understand the landscape well.

2: Figure Out Your Type

There are many types of copywriters nowadays. As such, it is only fair that if you want to become a successful copywriter, you have to figure out the type you would like to be. There are copywriters who deal primarily in SEO, those who deal in print advertising media only, those that produce content of all sorts and those who are focused on web editing mainly. There are many other types of copywriters; the above are just a few of the many.

You need to find out the type you would like to be in order to gather enough information about it, develop the necessary skills and venture successfully into it. If you are just venturing into copywriting, it would be wise to begin with content writing. This involves writing all sorts of materials from website content to e-books to magazine articles to promotional content. However, if you find it difficult to produce good quality content of all sorts, it is best to pick a type and stick to it. Find out more about the types of copywriting here.

Once you have selected a type, find some renowned copywriters in that category and research on them. Try to get in touch with them if possible and request for their mentorship;

there is nothing as beneficial as having a mentor in the industry you want to succeed in. Therefore, find a mentor if you can and then get guidance from him/ her to succeed in your respective field. A mentor has already achieved things you are aspiring to have and can give you valuable guidance to become successful. If you cannot find a mentor, you may perhaps want to enroll in a copywriting course like this one. You can also find other courses here. On these platforms, you will find lots of valuable information that will hold you by the hand until you succeed.

3: Find the Particular Industry You Would Like to Venture in and Reach Out to People

Successful copywriters pick a particular industry they would like to venture in and familiarize themselves with the jargon, technicalities and trends related to it. This enables them to write amazing copies that 'don't sound off'. Think about writing copy for a tech company dealing with SaaS solutions; you are unlikely to write a good copy if you don't understand the industry well so that you can carefully use words in a manner that gets customers wanting to click the buy, subscribe, bookmark or share button.

Therefore, if you wish to venture into a particular niche, find out which industry you would like to target and become an expert in it. For instance, if you like writing about food, you could target restaurants and hotels and present yourself as a copywriter who writes sales copies related to food and related services. If you feel you are more suited for the telecommunications industry, familiarize yourself with it and then reach out to companies in that industry.

However, this isn't mandatory. You can target as many industries as you like to increase your chances of getting good clients. Whether you decide to stick to one industry or step into many, start reaching out to people.

Luckily, with the advancement in internet, there exists various online forums that can help you get good clients e.g. Upwork, Fiverr, Freelancer, Craiglist and Guru. Create your profile on as many platforms as you can and then start sending proposals to the potential clients there. Each platform has its own procedure and rules so familiarize yourself with them first and then start applying for different job offers.

You will most likely be asked to submit a sample or two to showcase your skills to prospective customers so make sure to create your best copy to provide when needed. If you have any other written sample, attach it even if it is not a sales copy as it showcases your talent and the variation you can bring in your style. Most of the gigs (projects) that you will get from these platforms will be short-term projects. Clients may ask you to do one piece or more for a certain period for them. However, if a client is extremely pleased with your work, he/ she may return for more so make sure to give your best shot in each project.

In addition, check out the different companies you wish to work for on social media forums such as Facebook, LinkedIn and Twitter and get connected with them. Comment on their posts and interact as much as you can on their pages to show your interest in their work. Also, indirectly show your desire to work for/with them and leave them a message about it. However, make sure not to do that repeatedly because you may end up irritating the organization and getting blocked.

Also, get the word out about your new venture into copywriting; you can tell your friends, relatives and just about anyone who cares to give you an audience. Remember that before organizations can pay you to write their sales copy, you will need to attract people with your amazing content. The more you spread the word, the better will be your chances of finding more clients.

4: Create a Compelling Sales Pitch

When you apply for different copywriting projects, ensure to create a compelling sales pitch for each one of them. The people you are aiming to write for need to know why they should choose you and your sales pitch should provide them with all the reasons to pick only you. Discuss your passion for the job, any experience you have in the field, what you can bring to the table, how adept you are in the field, your commitment to your work and other qualities that will impress the prospective client(s).

However, make sure not to oversell yourself. On the reality cooking show 'Kitchen Nightmares', Gordon Ramsay, a renowned American chef always cut backs on the dishes included in the menu because he knows no chef can be an expert in hundreds of dishes. Similarly, you need to accept that you cannot be an expert at marketing, copywriting, social media and SEO at the same time.

As such, never oversell yourself and never write about things you haven't done or those you cannot do well because being dishonest about your skill set may get you a gig or two for now but it will never help you build a good reputation in the industry.

5: Practice and Practice Some More

As you send job proposals to different companies and individuals, don't forget to practice your writing skills. Find different samples of sales copies online and go through them to become more familiar with the work. Next, choose any random product you wish to promote and think of a catchy tagline or a theme you would like to work around.

Brainstorm as many ideas as you can to come with something innovative. When you have something interesting to work with, build up on the idea. Look for good vocabulary that brings out your message clearly and effectively. Remember, copywriters aren't word writers but word choosers. This means that your job won't be to just fill in words even when they don't mean anything, but to come up with some that adds value and substance to the copy so choose your words cautiously.

Your writing must have a clear message and lots of structure in it so go through your final piece a few times to ensure it does not lack substance. Also, be passionately involved in your writing. Think of yourself as that product's/service's customer and then think of what would compel you to make a purchase. Use that insight to come up with compelling content for the sales copy.

Carry out this practice as much as you can. Practice makes a man perfect. While nothing is perfect, things are good enough so practice as much as possible to become better at copywriting. Use your best pieces as samples to get better clients.

You can also consider taking a copywriting course and read as many books as you can on the topic because reading is one powerful way to learn and improve any skill.

6: Be Consistent

Like with everything else, consistency is the key to win. If you want to be a successful copywriter, you need to be consistent in your efforts. You need to practice consistently, reach out to people consistently and send proposals for job offers consistently as well. It may take you some time to land some big clients, but if you are consistent, you will definitely get there. You may have to start small in the start so be prepared to write good content on low rates for a while. On average, new and amateur writers in the U.S get $15 to $30 for a 500 words, but there are many writers who are willing to work for even lower rates. Since you don't have much experience in the field yet, you will have to face fierce competition from these writers so stay strong. If your work is good and you build a good rapport with a client, you will soon start commanding better rates as well.

Consistency is a good habit you will have to nurture to develop the copywriting skill and any other skill as a matter of fact. To build this skill, do the following:

- First, start talking positively to yourself. Often, we find it difficult to do things we are not used to doing or the tough tasks or anything out of the ordinary, because we don't believe in ourselves. If you look closely, you will realize that your negative beliefs about your abilities are deeply rooted in your negative self-talk. Your self-talk refers to the way you talk to yourself (the internal/mental dialogue that you have about different issues in life) and if it is negative, chances are, you will find it difficult to set any meaningful goal for yourself, have an unwavering self-belief and build any skill you want. Hence, start talking nicely to yourself. Each time you say anything disparaging to yourself, 'catch yourself' doing that and change it to something more positive. If you think 'I can never be a six figure copywriter' or 'It is too hard to practice every day', change it to 'If I try, I am sure I'll be a great copywriter who earns 6 figures' or 'Practicing writing is fun if I become involved in it so today, I'll become more engaged in my practice session.' Do this as much as possible and soon, you'll train yourself to engage in positive self-talk only. This will slowly help you nurture a positive mindset which will make it easier for you to become consistent and build important skills.

- Set a certain time of the day to practice your skill. Try to do this task during this time only to cultivate regularity and punctuality. Begin with practicing for 20 minutes and slowly increase the time to 30, 40 and 60 minutes. Do take short breaks after working for 20 minutes so you don't over-exhaust yourself.

- Set nice rewards for yourself that you can indulge in once you are done with the practice session. This reinforces positive behavior and helps you become consistent in building the respective skill.

Practice these steps daily and soon, you'll find yourself improving your skill set. The same steps should be used to nurture other skills that will be discussed in this book. Let us move to the next skill- coding that can set you on the path to a six figure income.

Chapter 3: Skill #2- Coding

Code is the language of the future. In fact, Fastcompany.com considers coding the most important skill of the future. That's for sure, especially given that we are increasingly becoming technology dependent. From the phones we use to the computers we have in our offices to the vehicles, home entertainment systems, to home automation systems to our security systems to our offices, to transportation, telecommunication, aviation, and much more, technology is at the center of the future of humanity. This perhaps explains why coding is regarded as one of the most sought after skill in today's work environment with 8/25 of the top 25 jobs on Glassdoor being tech positions. And it is not just in the technology sector, there is an increasing number of businesses and individuals relying on computer code. Job positions that require coding as a skill also command higher wages. And the good thing is that with this skill, you are just not going to work in the tech industry; coding is now needed in literally every area of the economy including health care, finance, banking, education and even art.

But what exactly does this skill entail? Let's discuss that.

Coding is the skill that helps us create applications, websites and software. Your operating system, browser, gaming console, home automation system, apps on your mobile phone, the website/device you are using now and all the social media forums you are a member are all made using coding skills.

A code is simply a language that a computer can understand. Just like humans need a language to communicate with other humans and in their mind, so do computers. But since computers don't use the same language as us humans, we have to input a message that they can understand in order for them to execute different functions. Machines/computers can only understand other machines/computers. And without the necessary mechanism of transferring what's being communicated by computers, humans cannot 'decode' the message. I want you to think of code as a way of translating between 2 normal languages. For instance, think of Chinese and English for instance; there is no way someone who has never learned Chinese can understand it if they are English speakers and vice versa. Therefore, if a Chinese man and English man need to know what the other wants, they have to involve a translator/interpreter. The work of the interpreter in this case would be to pick the message in one language, understand it well then pass the same message to the other side, of course in a different language. Your work as a coder would be to make computers to do whatever it is that you want to do. Computers understand in zeros and ones. Computers can understand only two types of data: one and off since it is a collection of many on and off switches known as transistors. Everything computers do is nothing more than a special combination of certain transistors turned off and some left on.

These combinations are represented as 1s and 0s which is known as the binary code. Every digit in the code symbolizes one transistor. The binary code is then grouped into bytes, which are group of 8 digits, each digit representing one transistor so there are 8 transistors in total. The modern computers today comprises of millions of transistors. Since writing a computer program by simply typing out millions of 0s and 1s is difficult for us, we use code to create a language that computers can understand. There are different programming languages designed to write the binary codes. A coding or programming language is a set of rules that define the right way to write and format a computer code. There are scores of programming/coding languages that help us craft many different websites, application and computer software. These languages allow us to write a code faster without having to write the binary code since the languages translate the input to a binary code.

Now that you have a good understanding of what coding is, let us take a look into its importance.

Why You Need to Build this Skill

A report from Burning Glass, a renowned firm that specializes in creating job market analytics shows that in 2015, there were around 7 million job openings in the country that demanded applicants to have coding skills. The report also shows that programming related jobs are growing at a 12% rate as compared to other skills in the market. Moreover, coding skills are needed in different job categories such as data analysts, scientists, engineers, information technology (IT) worker, designers and artists. It also found out that programming languages such as HTML, JavaScript, Python and C++ were quite in demand.

The report collected data from around 26 million online job postings in the U.S. All its findings prove that coding is indeed a core skill that help bolster your chances of earning a high salary. There are many coding related jobs that pay around $22,000 or more per year and around 49% of coding related jobs pay over $58,000 annually. That's not all; there are many coders who are earning 6 figures easily by creating different applications, websites and software.

According to BLS, coding related jobs will grow by 18.8% until 2024 which shows that coding will definitely be a sought after skill years from now so if you start working on it now, you will be quite adept it in the future.

Moreover, coding is a skill that can bring some other benefits some that can help you directly in making six-figure income. If you know how to code, you can easily design a website for yourself or for the business that you are running; you can create applications for laptops and smartphones; and you can even create new software.

Now that you are better aware of the importance of learning this skill, let us take a look at how you can learn it.

There is no right or wrong method to learn coding, but here are a few good places to start with for beginners.

1: Pick a Language You Want to Learn

There are many programming languages and while it is good to learn as many as possible because each of them has its own pros, you cannot learn all in the start. Hence, pick one that you would like to start with based on what you plan to do. For instance, if you wish to write an iOS app, begin learning Swift. If you want to learn an advanced level language, opt for Python, as it is the most sought after programming language. You can check the comparison of some popular coding languages here.

Before you pick a language, do think about what you wish to do so you can start off with something that helps fulfill your current objective.

2: Start Small and Understand the Basics

A good place to start learning coding is to start small and grasp the basics first. David Sinsky is a self-taught popular coder who learned to code in just 8 weeks. He began with getting an introduction of Python and spent a weekend understanding it only before moving forward. He advises all the people trying to learn coding to do the same- always start small with the basics, break the tasks into smaller steps and then gradually move forward.

3: Use Training Sites, Take Courses, Read Books

There are lots of free online training websites such as Codeacdemy, KhanAcademy and Code.org that provide free tutorials that can help you learn coding. There are also paid courses too that can help you learn coding easily. Research on them online and you'll find lots of courses to suit your needs. Before opting for one, do check reviews and only choose those with good reviews.

Additionally, read books on the subject to help you build sufficient understanding of different concepts on the subject. For instance, there is an enormous collection of around 500 free programming books on GitHub and you can also check out this collection of e-books on 24 coding languages.

4: Use a Kid's App

There are some fantastic coding apps for kids nowadays too. They are simple to understand and use, and are even suitable for all ages. Scratch is one good example of a coding app for kids that is suitable for adults too. Use it when starting out to practice what you learn and as you progress, you can move on to creating your own apps.

5: Practice What You Learn and Play Coding Games

The value of practice cannot be overemphasized. And what better way to practice than to play games; you learn while having fun, right? A good way to make practice sessions fun is to play coding games such as CodinGame and Code Combat.

Focus on these steps and practice them consistently to learn this skill. To ensure you learn it effectively and make the right use of it, break the habit of procrastination. Here is how you can do that.

Building the Habit of Taking Action on Time

To become successful in whatever you do, you need to overcome your urge to procrastinate and start taking action on time. Here is how you can do that.

- First, analyze the harmful effects of procrastination on your life and see how it is keeping you from living your dream life. This will encourage you to break it for good.

- Create your daily to-do list the night before to ensure you are prepared for the next day beforehand.

- Check the first task on the list in the morning and do it without overthinking it. Whatever it is you are supposed to do, just take the first step and if that seems difficult, try the 5 minute hack. Set a timer for 5 minutes and commit to work on a task for only 5 minutes and keep doing that until you complete 20 to 30% of that job. Practice this consistently and soon, you'll nurture the habit to do stuff on time.

- Also, do a task the minute you assign it to yourself so you don't postpone it.

- Reward yourself when you do take action and perform a task on time to reinforce this positive behavior.

Tip: Talk nicely to yourself especially when you have a slip-up and you will soon be able to effectively overcome procrastination when the urge to postpone tasks comes knocking.

With another important skill covered, let us move to the 3rd skill that can help you earn in 6 figures- online marketing.

Pursue Your Passion E-book

Chapter 4: Skill #3- Online Marketing

The internet has made the concept of global village a reality. With over 3 billion people now having access to the internet, the huge market created by the internet is something that businesses the world over have to find innovative ways to take advantage of. That's where the internet/online marketing skill is increasingly demanded.

What is Online Marketing?

Online marketing is simply a set of tools and methods that are used for promoting products and services through the internet. It (Online marketing) involves identifying the right type of online marketing mix that will appeal to your respective target market and will help turn potential customers into actual customers. A lot of analysis and research goes into selecting the marketing mix as well as measuring how successful each strategy proves to be. There are different methods/approaches of online marketing some of which include the following:

- Search Engine Marketing: This encompasses search engine marketing

(SEM) and SEO (search engine optimization). SEO helps improve the ranking of your business website in the search engine listing in a bid to increase organic traffic to your website and improves the chances of sales. SEM is the paid search marketing. You pay a certain fee to search engines and they display your advertisement on the user's search results whenever he/ she searches using any of your keywords. SEM statistics help provide good feedback on your ad's effectiveness.

- Mobile Marketing: Mobile marketing refers to advertising services and goods to people who are using mobile devices like smartphones and tablets. With advancement in technology, you can target people who are using mobile devices to see certain ads on different platforms. This can greatly improve conversions given that a <u>huge part of the access to the internet these days is from mobile devices</u>. Mobile marketing also involves push notifications, SMS marketing etc.

- Email Marketing: When you build a mailing list of people who are likely to want to buy your products or services, you can use email marketing to generate leads and sales. All you will need to do is to send your subscribers emails about your current products/services, keep them up-to-date with the latest promotions and deals, and inform them of any upcoming events. You can even send weekly/monthly newsletters and special offerings to them via email. This keeps your potential customers involved in your business and improves the conversion rate (when a potential customer becomes an actual customer.)

- Online Advertising: There are lots of different types of advertisement options available online such as banner ads, displaying webpages before or after reaching an expected website, text ads and social media ads.

- Social Media Marketing: Social media sites such as Pinterest, Facebook, Twitter, Instagram and LinkedIn are great platforms for marketing goods and services. With these platforms, all you need to do is to create your business account/page and then create interesting posts, videos and other content to draw your target market towards it to increase engagement.

- Blogging: Blogging is a powerful way to promote a business, as it engages the audience, get feedback and much more. You can blog about your product/service, latest trends in the industry or inform them about interesting and upcoming promotions and events to attract them towards your work.

Now that you have a basic understanding of what online marketing entails, let us talk about its importance so you know why you need to work on this skill.

Importance of Online Marketing

1: The market is huge

According to the sales forecasts by eMarketer, e-commerce sales will most probably reach up to $4.058 trillion across the globe by 2020. This whopping figure reflects the ever-increasing trend of online shopping and proves that online marketing is indeed a skill worth building. This presents an opportunity for anyone with great online marketing skills to help those who want to sell online.

Another survey published in 2016 shows that around 54% consumers purchase products online on a monthly or weekly basis. This figure will most likely increase by 2020. This is applicable to most of the industries.

So if the majority of your customers will be making online purchases, it is important to work on building your online marketing skills to ensure you reach out to those who are actually looking for various products and make a sale. You can offer online marketing services to corporates or you can use these skills to market your business, products or services. Since most of your competitors are likely to have an online presence, you too need to jump in the bandwagon then use your online marketing skills to have an edge over the competition, which ultimately enables you to increase your market share.

2: Affordable

You cannot compare the cost of online marketing with offline e.g. print or radio/TV advertising! This is great if you are running a marketing campaign for your business since you won't need to spend a lot of money on advertising. It is also great if you are being hired as an online marketing professional, as

you can help your customers to keep marketing
costs low while of course ensuring the returns
on investment is high.

3: Targeting

The internet provides a wide array of complex
tools for performing literally everything. For
instance, there are tools for targeting people
that meet a certain criteria (e.g. age, gender,
geographical location, preferences etc.) so that
you can market products/services to them and
tools that you can use to measure performance
to determine the effectiveness of your
marketing campaigns. This ensures you can
easily tweak what needs to be tweaked to attain
whichever goals you may be having. This is not
possible with offline advertising i.e. print, radio
and TV. This very feature ultimately ensures
that you have more control over your
marketing efforts, budget and literally
everything about your products/brand.

As you can see, if you run your own business, it
is imperative to work towards building this skill.
Even if you don't have your own business, you
should still consider building this skill because
it broadens your horizon and can helps you
become an online marketer for other firms.
Having online marketing as an added skill

commands higher salary in many job positions these days so you shouldn't overlook it.

So how exactly can you develop the skill? Here is how:

How to Learn Online Marketing

Try the following steps and strategies to become a good online marketer.

1: Start Surfing the Web

If you are not much acquainted with the internet, start familiarizing yourself with different online advertising media such as banner ads and online marketplaces like eBay, Amazon and Craiglist.

2: Create Accounts on Different Social Media Platforms

Also, start building a social media presence by creating your accounts on the different social media sites listed above. It is not necessary to have a presence on all of them but targeting as many as possible is good as it increases your chances of attracting the attention of more people towards. Begin with having a presence on one or two social networks and gradually build your way up.

3: Enroll For A Marketing Course e.g. A Degree On Online Marketing

If you have the budget and time, I'd recommend that you pursue a course in online marketing such as a diploma or a degree to help you build a strong foundation that sets you up for massive success.

If you cannot enroll for formal training, you could enroll for specific internet marketing courses to help you get your footing. You can check out some of the courses on HubSpot or Google.

4: Familiarize Yourself with Internet Analysis

Being able to carry out analysis is essential if you want to become a pro at online marketing. You need to know how to analyze the market and its response towards different strategies to become more aware of its needs so you can incorporate the right strategies in your online marketing plan.

For that, you need to first determine who your target market is. First, be clear on what good or service you will be selling or marketing if you just plan to be a marketer and not the business owner yourself. Once you are clear on who your target market is, find out what percentage of them buys stuff online. Also, find out the platform they use most to find the product. This knowledge will help you to understand where you will sell the product in order to create more awareness about the product you are marketing. For instance, if you are targeting teenage girls who use Facebook and Instagram mostly, you need to have an active presence on these platforms if you really want to generate leads and perhaps make some sales.

Also, determine your major online competitors so you know how they work and market their goods/ services and the size of their online market share. You can do that by signing up for their newsletters, researching their press releases and determining their weaknesses and strengths through their social media accounts, website and blog. You can even purchase an item or two from them to better understand their sales process.

5: Interpret the Gathered Data and Create a Strategy

Next, create reports with the help of Google Analytics, spreadsheets or any other good software using the data you have gathered. Use your reports and the results to create a successful marketing strategy that helps you to better reach your target market. Whatever your strategy is, you will need to create some content for it. If you have developed the copywriting skill that we discussed earlier, you won't have much trouble in creating written content on your own. However, if you don't have a lot of time to get the work done and want to create other types of content like infographics, you can hire freelancers from the different freelancing sites mentioned above such as Upwork.com, Freelancer.com, Fiverr.com etc.

Once you have a strategy, implement it and use Google Analytics to determine its effectiveness since this is the only way to figure out your ROI (return on investment). Analyze your strengths and weaknesses and then bring changes to your strategy accordingly to enhance its effectiveness.

As you work on these strategies to become better at online marketing, do build the habit of interacting with people and making more and better social networks.

Next, we will discuss why this is important:

Networking is an essential skill if you want to
succeed in any profession. However, its
importance increases if you are trying to
increase sales through online marketing.
Naturally, the more people you know, the
better will be the chances of more people
getting connected with your business and
skyrocketing its sales.

Also, having more people in your social
network helps you to build strong valuable
contacts that can help you to attain different
goals, which you wouldn't attain if you didn't
have a large social network. For instance, if you
know someone who is good at creating websites
or knows coding, you can learn the skill from
him/ her for free or at a discount, or ask them
to create your business website for free or at a
special price. Not only that, but by knowing
more people, you get a chance to know their
social networks better too and leverage them in
the hour of need.

To build this good habit, you have to start
reaching out to all the people you know on
different social media sites and even otherwise.
Have some quick chitchat if you can so you

understand what it is they could be expecting from your brand or you as a person. Just sharing what you do to everyone who cares to listen or pay attention is a good first step, as it will undoubtedly open opportunities referrals. For instance, if you reach out to your friends on various networks and tell them that you are an online marketing expert, some may want to give you jobs to help them get their businesses off the ground, some may want you to train them for a fee, some may want to refer you to their friends etc. This ultimately benefits you more than you could have imagined.

The fourth skill that can help you earn in six figures is being great at closing sales. The next chapter talks about it.

DOWNLOAD YOUR FREE BONUS:

Pursue Your Passion E-book

Chapter 5: Skill #4- Build Great Selling Skills

Life is about selling; we are always selling ourselves in one way or the other. Whether you are selling yourself to prospective spouses, employers, clients or customers, you are always selling yourself- it doesn't matter whether there is monetary consideration to the process. If you sell yourself short, you can be sure that you will definitely not get as many benefits as you would if you were good at it. That's why it is important to be purposeful about building the selling skill if you want to convert it to a moneymaking skill.

To earn 6 figures, you need to take your work to the next level. Whether you are running your own business or working for someone else, if you are good at selling, you can easily use this skill to earn big bucks fast. Before discussing this skill, let us quickly establish the difference between sales and marketing so you don't confuse the two as often, both the terms are used interchangeably which makes them difficult to understand.

Marketing refers to promoting goods and services and bringing them closer to the target market. Selling, on the other hand refers to actually selling those goods and services i.e. closing deals to move the customer from a prospective customer to a real customer. The job of a marketer is to carry out research on a certain service or product, explore its target markets, map out the price points based on different business factors, brand the services and goods, develop as well as analyze campaigns and then help the salespeople comprehend the unique selling proposition for every product. Salespeople take it up from there. A salesperson serves as the connection between a marketer and the potential customers. A salesperson actually sells the product to the potential customers and uses his/her knowledge of the product as well as knowledge about the target market's needs and demographics to lure potential customers towards a good or service and then make a sale.

Since you don't need to directly speak to the customer in online marketing, you work as both a salesperson and marketer when carrying it out. However, if you are physically selling a product or have a physical presence of your business, you need to build good selling skills.

Why is this skill important? Let's discuss that:

Good salesman ship is important for a number of reasons.

Firstly, it helps you get directly in touch with the potential customers and draw their attention towards the product. If you are good at selling stuff, you will easily grasp the attention of potential customers and turn them into actual customers.

If you are running your own business, building this skill is important so you can then hire and train others to effectively sell your products/ services as your business expands. Even if you are not running your own business, but are working in the sales department or any other department of a company, you need to know how to sell things. If you are in the sales department, selling is your job and being good at it will naturally increase chances of your promotion and success. However, if you are in some other department, having good selling skills will help you increase your popularity in the firm and come in the limelight. When people spread the word that they purchased a product or got to know of a business because of you, you will earn more recognition in the company and this will undoubtedly put you perfectly on the path to six figure income.

Not only that, but good sales skills help you sell your talents and skills better too. If you know the art of selling, you can easily promote your skills and talents in a gathering and draw the attention of relevant people towards your work. For instance, if you are engaging with people who work at a big company and want to work as a copywriter for them, you need to convince them of your excellent capabilities. If you are a good salesperson, you will do this job successfully and bag good clients.

To cap it all, selling things effectively helps you progress better in different areas of your business. Let us find out how you can build and improve this skill.

How to Become a Good Salesperson

Here are some effective ways to build good selling skills.

1: Be Clear on Your Mission

Start off by clarifying your mission. What niche do you want to venture in? What will you sell? Who is your target market and what are their needs? How can your product/service satisfy their needs? How much does your target market earn? What is your professional goal?

Answer these questions to better understand your goal and mission in life. This shouldn't just be when identifying your sales mission, but also your goals in different aspects of your life. Successful people across the world have the habit of setting clear and meaningful goals for themselves. This is precisely what helps them understand their goals, become passionate about them and then actively pursue such goals. Therefore, you need to figure out exactly what you want in different areas of your life such as health, wealth, abundance, fitness, spirituality, love etc. and then set meaningful goals based on those findings. This will help you to clearly understand your wants and needs, and then pursue them.

Therefore, spend quality time with yourself every day and analyze your deepest and genuine desires, interests, likes, passions and

strengths to better understand what you want
and then pursue it.

2: Set Specific Sales Goals

Once you are clear on your sales related
mission, break it down into yearly, monthly,
weekly and daily goals so you know exactly
what you should sell every day to fulfill your
mission. Your goals should be results based
such as sales per month, profit per sale,
amount per sale etc. so they can help you
measure your progress easily.

3: Understand Your Customers' Needs

Find out what your target market wants from
your product/service to better understand its
need. Engage with your potential customers on
a regular basis through social media, through
email or by calling them if you can. Also,
conduct surveys to find out what your target
market expects from your business or why they
prefer your competitor's product/ service over
yours.

4: Have a Compelling Sales Pitch

Create a striking sales pitch that focuses on the
importance and benefits of your
product/service and how it can solve a
particular problem or fulfill the need of your

target market. Practice that pitch as much as you can and make sure it is concise and to-the-point. Next, start delivering it whenever you feel you are around someone who may be interested in your product/service.

Also, increase your social networks because the more people you know, the better will be your chances of making more sales.

Another skill that is worth building is being good at managing teams. The next chapter throws light on it.

Chapter 6: Skill #5- Having Good Management Skills

Let's be honest, pulling six figures a month without needing any help from anybody is not going to be easy. In fact, it is bad practice if you shoulder all the burden. What if you get sick or are just not able to get the work done for one reason or another; does that mean you will make zero income? That's where teams come in.

Whether you are running your own business or working for someone, if you have good team management skills, you can easily take your business to the next level, improve its overall performance and sales, and start earning 6 figures.

Let's find out right here why you need to build good team management skills and how you can achieve this goal.

The Need to Build Good Management Skills

Management skills are all the skills that help you manage your team members and those working under or around you effectively. If you are a good manager, you understand your team better and can work as a good liaison between them and your superiors.

When you effectively communicate what clients, bosses and other stakeholders want, this makes it easy for those working under you to take appropriate action to do what needs to be done in the manner in which it should be done. The fact that there is clear communication eliminates ambiguity and confusion, which ultimately keeps everyone happy. The same applies if you are running your own business. Being able to understand your team helps you exploit their strengths better and keep them more engaged in their work.

Moreover, good management skills help you resolve problems easily and guide your team in an effective manner. You ensure everyone is on the same page with you and take each member together as a team to make them work zealously for you or your company. This improves the overall performance of the organization.

If you too want your business or the company you are working for to become better than ever, you must purpose to build/improve your management skills. How do you do that? Here is how:

To become better at managing teams, you first need to know the members in your team. Only when you know your team, can you understand the needs, potentials and qualities of different members. Finding out their needs helps you know what they are seeking from your company so you can help them reach their goals, which ultimately helps them to feel more motivated to give their best to the organization. Becoming aware of their talents, skills and potentials helps you know of their personal assets that you can exploit successfully and make your team members more involved in your work.

Secondly, you need to start engaging with your team members as much as you can. Talk to them in the workplace and even outside of it to build a good rapport with them. The more comfortable they are talking to you, the easier it will be for you to influence them and make them work effectively for you.

Thirdly, you need to communicate your concerns and message to them effectively. The key to doing that is to inform them of their responsibilities so they know what is expected of them and how a certain project is expected to grow.

Fourthly, you need to lead by example by practicing what you preach. If you ask your team members to do a certain thing or behave a certain way, you must do that yourself. When your team sees you practicing what you preach, they are likely to follow your example.

As you become a better manager and build good management skills, you could create courses on team management or give lectures to prospective and budding managers to improve their management skills. This will help you use your management skills to earn some good side income and improve your chances of earning six figures. If you do venture into this, building good public skills will definitely help you out. The next chapter elaborates on that.

Chapter 7: Skill #6- Build Effective Public Speaking Skills

Renowned public speakers like Tony Robbins, Jack Canfield and Brian Tracy earn millions of dollars each year with the help of their public speaking skills. Besides these brilliant speakers, there are many people who make hundreds of thousands of dollars through public speaking.

What does it entail? And why is it important to build the skill anyway? Let's discuss that:

Public Speaking and its Importance

Public speaking is simply that; speaking in public/before an audience regarding a certain topic of interest to the audience. While you may not perceive it to be a million dollar making skill, this skill can most certainly help you reach your goal of financial abundance and prosperity. If you are good at public speaking, you can become a keynote speaker and speak at different institutes. Keynote speakers usually earn anywhere between $10,000 and $100,000 for just a one hour lecture. Even if you are earning around $5,000 per every keynote, you only need about 20 bookings to earn 6 figures annually.

However, to reach this point, you will first need to take public speaking seriously and build good speaking skills.

Moreover, you can speak in seminars and workshops, and even give public speaking training sessions to increase your income. You can also create your own products and sell them to further boost up your income. For instance, Brain Tracy has created many public speaking programs and makes thousands of dollars each year by selling them. Tony Robbins is known to organize 'A Date With Destiny', which he charges over $5000 per person for attendance.

In addition, you can also give coaching lessons to other speakers especially the budding speakers to help them improve their skill and make some more money through this venture. However, this will only be possible when you have earned enough recognition and popularity through public speaking.

Here is how you can build this skill.

How to Become a Good Public Speaker

To become an excellent public speaker, first narrow down on a topic you would like to speak about. You need to have a certain area of expertise that you can speak effectively on. Unless you figure that out, it is likely you won't have a clear public speaking goal and strategy and won't be able to find your true voice. For instance, Tony Robbins is a motivational speaker and his job is to motivate people to be better. Similarly, Grand Cardone is a huge sales giant who ventured into public speaking some time back. He talks mainly about how to become a good salesman and that's his area of expertise.

Similarly, you have to find out what you are passionate about because if you are truly passionate about something, you will find it effortless to speak on it and improve your knowledge about that area.

Secondly, find your target market so you can research better on its needs and requirements. Next, you need to set your fee. Find out what your competitors are charging for an hour long talk to set a suitable price for your speaking engagements.

Next, you need to look for good speaking venues or engagements where you can meet people and speak to them. This helps you make more contacts and use them to sell your service better or to convince them of what you talk about. As you have more funds to rent halls and other venues to hold seminars, speaking events and workshops, start creating your events so you can sell your knowledge to people. Also, work on building your online presence so you can reach out to more people (you could for instance create a YouTube channel to help you to generate leads for you speaking engagements).

The seventh skill you should consider building is graphic designing. The last chapter of the book talks about it.

<u>Pursue Your Passion E-book</u>

Chapter 8: Skill #7- Learn Graphic Designing

Graphic design is the science and art of creating and arranging different text and images to communicate a certain message. It can be applied in different media such as digital, print, motion picture, product decoration, animation, signs and packaging. It is one of the most trending skills nowadays and is definitely one that can help you earn six figures.

I know you might be wondering; why is this skill so important anyway? Let's discuss that:

Importance of Graphic Designing

It is quite common for graphic designers these days to make anywhere between $35,000 and $65,000 annually. This amount increases as your experience and expertise improves. In fact, there are many successful graphic designers who are earning 6 figures per year, as employees in various companies and as freelancers.

Moreover, you can also teach graphic designing when you become good at it and hold seminars to earn extra income. If you are running your own business, graphic designing can help you create a good layout and design of your business website as well as more creative designs for your products and services.

Here is how you can become a skilled graphic designer.

How to Build the Graphic Designing Skill

Here are a few ways to build and improve your design skills.

- You could take different online tutorials and courses to learn the art of graphic designing and improve this skill. Here are some great tutorials that you can follow to learn graphics designing.

- Read lots of design books and follow different graphics design blogs to become up-to-date with the latest trends and to improve your knowledge of this skill. Designrfix, Gainbuzz, DesignTaxi and Artwork Abode are some good design blogs that can teach you how to build and improve this skill. A few good design books to begin with are: The Elements of Typographic Style by Robert Bringhurst, Graphic Design Theory: Readings from the Field by Helen Armstrong and 100 Ideas that Changed Graphic Design by Steven Heller. In addition, work on building the habit of reading good informational and how-to books regularly. Reading is one good habit all accomplished people possess that has helped them earn millions of dollars.

- As you learn the basics of graphic design, create some designs and create your portfolio or a few samples to show potential clients. And as you do that, make sure to practice as much as possible to enhance your skill.

- To take it a notch higher, create your profile on different online platforms like Upwork.com, Fiverr.com, Freelancer.com, 99designs.com etc. (these have been mentioned earlier on in the book) then apply for different graphics design jobs.

Work on these tips, stay consistent in your work and interact more with people to increase your chances of finding better, bigger clients.

DOWNLOAD YOUR FREE BONUS:

Pursue Your Passion E-book

Conclusion

We have come to the end of the book. Thank you for reading and congratulations for reading until the end.

I hope this book provided you with the value you were looking for and helps you achieve your goal of earning a 6 figure income.

If you found the book valuable, can you recommend it to others? One way to do that is to post a review on Amazon.

Click here to leave a review for this book on Amazon!

Thank you and good luck!

www.ingramcontent.com/pod-product-compliance
Lightning Source LLC
Chambersburg PA
CBHW071258220526
45468CB00001B/187